T0326363

The White Ribbon

German Film Classics

Series Editors

Gerd Gemünden, Dartmouth College
Johannes von Moltke, University of Michigan

Advising Editors

Anton Kaes, University of California-Berkeley
Eric Rentschler, Harvard University

Editorial Board

Also in the series:

THE WHITE RIBBON

FATIMA NAQVI

CAMDEN HOUSE

First published 2020 by Camden House

Camden House is an imprint of Boydell & Brewer Inc.
668 Mt. Hope Avenue, Rochester, NY 14620, USA
www.camden-house.com
and of Boydell & Brewer Limited
PO Box 9, Woodbridge, Suffolk IP12 3DF, UK
www.boydellandbrewer.com

Cover image: The burning barn, one of the "strange accidents"
that occurs in *The White Ribbon*. Courtesy of Wega Film /
Les Films du Losange / X Filme; Collection of Austrian
Filmmuseum.

ISBN-13: 978-1-64014-044-8
ISBN-10: 1-64014-044-1

Library of Congress Cataloging-in-Publication Data

CIP data applied for.

This publication is printed on acid-free paper.
Printed in the United States of America.

Publication of this book was supported by a grant from the
German Film Institute (GFI) of the University of Michigan
Department of Germanic Languages & Literatures.

CONTENTS

ACKNOWLEDGMENTS

Even little books require lots of help. I have had great interlocutors along the way. Roland Fischer-Briand, the archivist formerly in charge of Haneke's *Vorlass* at the Austrian Filmmuseum, sifted through boxes of material with me, and I fondly think back to conversations with him as well as his colleague, Paolo Caneppele. I am grateful to the audiences who have listened to me talk about Haneke over the years at Rutgers (*Danke*, Eva Erber!), Washington University (Lutz Koepnick), Duke (Kata Gellen), as well as in Strasbourg (Valérie Carré), Vienna (Markus Kupferblum), Regensburg (Bernhard Dotzler), Munich (Evelyn Annuß, Christian Innerhofer), Berlin (Christoph Holzhey and Manuele Gragnolati), and Bochum (Rupert Gaderer, Natalie Binczek, Armin Schäfer). A thank you goes to all the members of the Rutgers-Bochum Summer Academy 2018—as well as the students of my seminars at Harvard in spring 2018 and Yale in 2020. My gratitude goes to John Hamilton; his erudition finds its way into the closing section and into work yet to come. A special thanks goes to my close friend Roy Grundmann, with whom I have been talking about Haneke since 2008 and who kindly commented on not one, but two drafts. Finally, a great debt of gratitude goes to Michael Haneke himself, for his support over the years. We first met when I was a graduate student in the 1990s. With characteristic generosity, he then offered me a videocassette of *Three Paths to the Lake* (1976), a film I discuss here.

So why *The White Ribbon*? I feel drawn to this film for numerous reasons, but one stands out in particular. In interviews, the director discussed the film's telescoping of various moments of ideological indoctrination. He spoke of fascism, but also German left-wing radicalism associated with the Red Army Faction (RAF, also known as the Baader-Meinhof Group), as well as Islamic fundamentalism after 2001. His explanation was compelling for a number of personal reasons while also making me intellectually wary. Haneke melded three discrete eras I could trace through my own family history. My grandmother Margarete, born in 1904 near Stuttgart to a Berlin mother and Bohemian father, came from a strict, well-off household similar to the pastor's home in the film (she would, for instance, address her parents as "Herr Vater" and "Frau Mutter"). My parents, immigrants to New York City from Austria and Pakistan in the late 1960s, witnessed the euphoria and violence of the leftist movements to which Andreas Baader and Ulrike Meinhof belonged, part of a larger global student uprising against the conservative status quo and what was perceived as US neoimperialism in Vietnam. Finally, as a "hybrid" familiar with the rituals of Catholicism and the Shia Muslim faith as well as a denizen of post-9/11 New York, I wondered about the relationship between belief, indoctrination, and violence postulated in the film. Haneke's entangling of these components might be productive, but also calls for some unraveling. To do this disentangling, I have to thank my mother Brita, who followed the growth of this manuscript through its many permutations, and my sister Elia, who engaged with its argumentative twists. I never wrote without thinking about what my father Mohsin would have said about Haneke's views.

I adumbrated some of the ideas developed here in *Trügerische Vertrautheit: Filme von Michael Haneke*, which appeared with Synema Verlag in Vienna in 2010. Images from the storyboards are reproduced courtesy of Michael Haneke; stills are courtesy of Wega Film / Les Films du Losange / X Filme Creative Pool and are drawn from the Austrian Film Museum Collection.

This book is for Rick Rentschler, my first film teacher and a model mentor!

The White Ribbon

Introduction

Michael Haneke's films undermine certainties, activate critical thinking skills, reveal the fragmentary and contingent nature of the world and how we think about it: these have become truisms in discussions of his oeuvre. Perhaps a less common way of interpreting his works would be to emphasize that they are self-reflexive about being self-reflexive. They are inordinately "meta." Haneke's films reflect critically on the way in which we work through the past and reveal how hard it is to grapple with historical legacies, especially in a media-saturated age. They make apparent the blockages in memory, and they demonstrate the value of media artifacts like photographs in overcoming these obstructions. His works showcase our unconscious resistance to accountability. They also thematize our conscious problems with this resistance, especially when we have been trained to see it as morally repugnant. We have come to accept that it is imperative to work through the past, especially National Socialism. However, Haneke's films also suggest that being enjoined to "never forget" might be less emotionally effective than allowing ourselves to always be haunted—haunted by images of many pasts that ghost through our minds.

Haneke's acclaimed 2009 film *The White Ribbon* (*Das weiße Band*) brings together these various aspects. It engages with our response to Germany's traumatic twentieth-century history, especially after the end of the analog era. This black-and-white digital film has been seen as many things: a family drama, a whodunit, a film-festival darling, and an example of successful art-house cinema. It is also a morality tale, mind game, study on the function of media, and "heritage film with a vengeance."[1] *The White Ribbon* can be placed in a German tradition of Enlightenment critique, where horror emerges from rationality. Furthermore, *The White Ribbon* focuses on practices of transmission, inscription, and recording on a personal and social level. It delves into child-rearing practices that impress themselves on the body and mind, from one generation to the next. The film looks at what we gain when something is lost in translation; it presses superimposition into the service of truthfulness, mixing historical trajectories (pre–World War I Germany, Nazism, left terrorism of the 1960s, Islamic radicalism post-2001). It thereby insinuates that an affecting amalgam of epochs may have epistemological benefits when we try to understand the internalization of ideology.[2] Viewers' knowledge arises from the figures' lack thereof; their recurrent line is: "I don't know." However, the film requires artistic effects to create the veneer of historical accuracy and artlessness, and it uses the digital tools about which it is skeptical to produce a sheen of epistemological truth. Laying out its mystery and challenging spectators to engage with it, *The White Ribbon* foregrounds the sensory limitations of film while also utilizing this medium to craft a sumptuous aesthetic feature. In 2009, it took home the Cannes Palme d'Or for Best Film, three European Film Awards, the FIPRESCI Grand Prize, and garnered Oscar nominations for Best Foreign Language Film and Best Cinematography. In 2010, it was awarded the Golden Globe for Best Foreign Language Film.

The *White Ribbon*'s seventy-eight scenes, shot in color but drained to black-and-white in post-production, take place in the year leading up to World War I. The events are confined to the village of Eichwald in Northern Germany. While the globe hurtles toward violent conflagration and four empires near their end (the Prussian, Russian, Austro-Hungarian and Ottoman), horrific events of a smaller magnitude occur in Eichwald: freak accidents, child beatings, and disappearances consume the village. The film compels us to extrapolate from small to large, part to whole; yet it doubts whether the locale can even stand in for the world at large. Is it legitimate to see Eichwald as a microcosm of militarism, nationalism, ethnic identity, and intolerance—or is it just one truly evil place sui generis? It is composed of a handful of local dignitaries such as the baron, the doctor, the estate steward, and the teacher. There is also the mass of impoverished farmers and farm hands. Its social structure is male-dominated, its economy quasi-feudal. The terrible happenings keep the villagers and viewers in carefully calibrated suspense, as a host of questions are raised but never answered. Who attached the trip wire that causes the doctor's horse to stumble and the doctor (Rainer Bock) to break his collarbone? Where did the pastor's children (Maria-Victoria Dragus, Martin Proxauf) vanish the same evening? Who is responsible for the death of the tenant farmer's wife in the crumbling saw mill? Who thrashed the baron's son (Fion Mutert) on the evening of the harvest festival, and who hurt the midwife's child with Down's syndrome (Eddy Grahl), damaging the latter's eyesight? Who set the barn on fire?

With the exception of a few misdeeds, no perpetrator is ever discovered. The camera catches the tenant farmer's son (Sebastian Hülk) *in flagranti*, as he destroys the baron's cabbage patch with a scythe as revenge for his mother's fatal plunge in the saw mill. The camera also espies the pastor's daughter as she grabs her father's pet bird from its cage and a sharp letter opener; two sequences later we see the dead bird arranged in the shape of the cross on the desk. And the steward's son throws the baron's effete child into the pond for playing a pretty fife.

These events unfold against the backdrop of tainted pedagogical practices and authoritarian familial structures. The pastor punishes his children repeatedly for their infractions against the Protestant moral code; the steward maltreats his son, who has stolen the small flute; the doctor sexually abuses his teenage daughter. Otherwise, the film's varied segments and the voice-over commentary only indicate currents of gossip and wild conjectures. For Eichwald's inhabitants, the God-given order—where misogyny and subjection, patriarchy and religiosity go hand in hand—seems derailed. For viewers, however, this order seems ripe for the harvest. Only nature appears unperturbed, and stunning landscape shots reveal its quietly disturbing beauty through the seasons.

The White Ribbon utilizes many authenticating effects to establish the truthfulness of its reconstruction, the veracity of its depiction of the past. The careful mise-en-scène, with its period costumes, detailed depiction of agricultural methods, and retro architecture (the shingle roofs artfully retouched), led me to Haneke's archive. I examined his production notes, script, story board, and posters at the Austrian Film Museum in order to think about what such a period film might accomplish. While it attempts to ground its truth claims in an extra-filmic reality that historical photographs vouchsafe, it mistrusts these efforts to substantiate truth-in-representation by recourse to something we might call verifiable history, a history that can be authenticated.

In looking at this tension between what we know and how we know it, I focus on Haneke's engagement with inscription. Haneke is an exacting director interested in every aspect of production, and his desire to work in Europe rather than the US is tied to this kind of control. As a result, his films evince a distinct "handwriting," and close analysis is fruitful for teasing out internal rhymes as well as stylistic and thematic connections within his oeuvre. In this book, I first discuss the filmmaker's ongoing relationship to Austrian literature. With *The White Ribbon*, Haneke inscribes himself in a modernist canon that deals idiosyncratically with World War I to offer an encompassing view of a culture in decline. His "literariness"— the invocation of literary conventions—in the film also draws on a longstanding poetic tradition, where a voluble narrator comments on events within the embedded story. While the frame in literature can have multiple functions, it here establishes authority, grounds the story in lived experience, and demonstrates the first-person narrator's intellectual investment and emotional distance.[3] It also introduces epistemological questions and smooths over narrative inconsistencies—to which I draw attention. Throughout the course of the film, Haneke's "literary" techniques remind viewers of the blank page necessary for inscription to occur. As the screen turns blindingly white in transitional scenes, the whiteness evokes an achromatic empty sheet of paper. Haneke, the filmmaker-turned-scribe, reverses the color's associations with innocence and incorruptibility, leaving a dark message in dazzling images. Posterity is asked to bear witness to events it cannot fully fathom or even discern.

Haneke is also writing himself into a historiographic, philosophical, and photographic tradition, not only a textual canon. *The White Ribbon* retraces 1960s and 1970s debates about the rise of fascism. In probing the ways in which pedagogy engraves its tenets on the minds and bodies of boys and especially girls within Protestantism, the film draws on Katharina Rutschky's groundbreaking compendium on "black pedagogy" from 1977.[4] Rutschky and others saw this detrimental child-rearing pedagogy as part and parcel of the Enlightenment and a precursor to authoritarianism. Furthermore, as a result of the student revolution of 1968, the gender politics of fascism were discussed in psychoanalytically inflected cultural studies (which I associate here with Klaus Theweleit); Haneke picks up on this discourse about women's roles. Finally, engaging with the aesthetic history of photographic portraiture, Haneke visualizes the tensions his film creates between a universalizing typology and the particularistic thrust of photography. From the beginning of his career, the filmmaker has problematized the ubiquity of images and their naturalization in contemporary experience.[5] Haneke returns to his 1976 adaptation of Ingeborg Bachmann's story "Three Paths to the Lake" (1972) to interrogate cinema's relation to photography as well as photography's ability to raise awareness about victimization and injustice.[6] The television film proffers what Susan Sontag terms an "ecology of images" via photography—and distinguishes Haneke's *praxis* from that of other directors. In its use of montage and portrait photography, *The White Ribbon* also summons up German photographer August Sander (1876–1964) and his vast atlas *People of the Twentieth Century*, published only in abridged form as *Face of Our Time* in 1929. Haneke alludes to Sander to reflect on what the building blocks of film might be, those *ur*-texts of visual practice determining how we visualize the past.[7] Referring to the individual cinematic image in the analog era, Haneke once said film tells falsehoods—at a rate of 24 frames per second.[8] This is even more true in the digital epoch, which exacerbates the tendency toward deception. Post-production with its special effects means that images do not rely on any grounding in the real world to come into existence. With the indexical relationship to the object world in front of the camera lens severed, film no longer functions as a historical archive. In other words, Haneke does not espouse the fantasy of the digital: the digital neither escapes "time, entropy, degradation," nor can "information [. . .] simply be transferred, without loss, from one 'medium' to another."[9] In the era of the digital archive, where the historical record can be manipulated or fabricated, *The White Ribbon* queries the status of the individual picture—if such a thing can even be discerned from within the stream of digital data.

The critique of media in relation to historical verifiability goes beyond the image to include sound in *The White Ribbon*. The audio track and the sense of hearing both receive sustained attention. The film sensitizes us to the "full potential of sound, pitch, and volume."[10] Until 2009, Haneke employed music to gesture toward the transcendent realm. In his early works, classical music functions as a repository of wholeness in contrast to the depleted televisual realm, the dominion of deceit and distortion. Alban Berg's violin concerto "To the Memory of an Angel" in *The Seventh Continent* (1989) and Bach's motet "Jesus, My Joy" in *Benny's Video* (1992) signal a utopian dimension unavailable to the families within the narratives. In both feature films, music's redemptive potential disrupts the plots' bleakness to serve as an authorial, extradiegetic interpolation in the characters' sorry lives. For brief interludes, classical music lends credibility to the youthful witness, be it the girl Eva in *The Seventh Continent* or the teenager Benny in *Benny's Video*.

In *The White Ribbon*, when the doctor's daughter (Roxanne Duran) tugs at her earlobe and strains to hear the chink of the pebbles thrown at her window, we should be alert: Haneke is extending his skepticism about the image to dialogue and ambient sound. We need to pay attention to the aural dimension, to the slightest perturbations in and of the air. While pierced ears take on a sexual dimension in regard to the young woman's molestation, penetration also pertains to sound's ability to transcend physical barriers (the children's beating behind closed doors) and link unconnected spaces via sound bridges (the various sites around the manor during the harvest festival). Indeed, the acoustic plane may be as potentially misleading as the visual image. Conflicting temporalities, for instance, are registered within the aged grain of the narrator's voice (Ernst Jacobi), which opens and closes the film. Although we never see him, we *hear* Jacobi's eighty-five years of age. The temporal disjunction between the "now" in which the film opens and the "then" in which the enframed story takes place (where the narrator speaks with the youthful voice of Christian Friedel) undermines the narrator's authoritative speaking position, as well as the immediacy with which he appeals to listeners. The film also probes our willingness to trust the sung word, the hymn. We may interpret Baroque music as being removed from the sphere of daily life and Paul Gerhardt's Lutheran hymn "Commit Thou All They Griefs" (Befiehl Du Deine Wege) as indicating redemption. However, choral music, too, belongs to the way of life and the system of beliefs *The White Ribbon* indicts.

Literariness

In the German-speaking world, adapting films from literature has many implications. It shores up the canon of the educated bourgeoisie, the *Bildungsbürgertum*. It implies the wish to write oneself into this literary tradition, which confers distinction and cultural capital. It means participating in the circulation of words for geopolitical reasons (after 1945, adaptations marked West Germany's superiority over the German Democratic Republic, for instance, as inheritors of a "true" German tradition and vice versa). For Haneke, the strategy of evoking literature serves another function: it elicits déjà-vu on the part of an intellectual audience familiar with famous books relating to the lead-up to war and its outbreak. Haneke thereby augments viewers' sense of inexorability and emphasizes the portentous nature of seemingly minor occurrences—they foreshadow the great cataclysm of World War I *and* World War II.

Since many of Haneke's films are based on well-known literature,[11] a mature work like *The White Ribbon* self-confidently plays with convention in serving up a faux screen adaptation. The director is interested in the pre-war period, when an "epoch lies on its deathbed," in the Austrian writer Karl Kraus's 1922 formulation.[12] Haneke previously explored this era in his sepia-tinted 1993 television film based on Joseph Roth's 1924 novel *Rebellion*, which begins with documentary footage of Emperor Franz Joseph's funeral, coastline invasions, battlefields, and trenches from various theaters of war.[13] The end of Austria-Hungary is also present in the 1997 TV adaptation of Franz Kafka's unfinished novel *The Castle* (1926), where confusion reigns in a waning, highly bureaucratic empire. *The White Ribbon* concentrates on the "last days of mankind," the subject of Kraus's acerbic play about the end of Austria-Hungary and the German Empire under Wilhelm II.[14] With representatives of all social strata in 1913, Haneke, like Kraus, offers us a world in miniature to indict blinkeredness, chauvinism, and aggression. A who's who of prestigious German-language actors is pressed into service to display the hierarchical makeup of society: a pastor (Burghart Klaußner), estate agent (Sepp Bierbichler), baron (Ulrich Tukur), and doctor (Rainer Bock) join the lower-ranking teacher (Christian Friedel), tutor (Michael Kranz), and farmer (Branko Samarovski). The baroness (Ursina Lardi), pastor's spouse (Steffi Kühnert), and steward's wife (Gabriela Maria Schmeide) complement the lowly nanny (Leonie Benesh), midwife (Susanne Lothar), and maid (Birgit Minichmayr). The narrator notes the impending cataclysm that the film does not ever show: "None of us expected it would be our last new year in an era of peace and that this year would bring radical change of a magnitude none of us could even remotely foresee." After the narrator marks the exact historical juncture as being December 1913, we hear the members of polite society make offhand references to imminent collapse. "The world won't come crashing down," the gentlemen from the upper class scoff repeatedly. The implosion of World War I does not lie within their horizon of expectation as it does in ours, whom the writings of Kraus, Roth, Kafka, Robert Musil, and Stefan Zweig have conditioned.

To conjure the illusory "world of security" before 1914—to quote a chapter title of Zweig's poignant memoir *The World of Yesterday: Memories of a European* (1941)[15]—is to convey just how unprepared this society is to meet challenges such as the multicultural fabric of everyday life (signaled by the influx of Polish workers) or the younger generation's resistance to authority. When a visibly shaken baron announces to his wife that the Austrian successor to the throne has been assassinated in Sarajevo, bibelots, wall tapestries, standing vases, and candelabras surround him (fig. 1). He appears as one antiquated thing among many, the untimely symbol of a disappearing world. Retrospectively, his aggressiveness turns out to have been inflated posturing, and his grip on power proves evanescent.

Christian Berger's Oscar-nominated cinematography and Monika Willi's editing (hewing closely to Haneke's storyboard) strengthen

Fig. 1. The baron and the "world of yesterday." Collection Austrian Filmmuseum.

the sense of a foreclosed future and make tangible the violence already present in the literary intertexts. Gruesome events take place chronologically in rapidly unfolding scenes, moving us from attempted murder to attempted suicide, from barn burning to sexual exploitation, from physical to verbal abuse. This ordering is unusual for Haneke, whose films generally scramble the sequencing to cast doubt on causality. To heighten the narrative suspense, the film pursues a visual strategy of containment that further augments tension. The precise framing within sequences makes palpable the bottled-up energy unable to erupt in open revolt (physical violence often takes place off screen). Medium close-ups and close-ups in the interior spaces, where many conversations take place, emphasize viewers' feelings of constriction. A slightly tilted camera makes visible power differentials in the shot/reverse shots used for dialogues within the rooms.[16] However, abrupt transitions between segments imply that the pent-up forces in Eichwald cannot be entirely suppressed, with frequent cuts in the middle of a physical action. Scenes occasionally appear "decapitated," with faces and heads invisible when a scene starts or ends. The film largely eschews tracking shots in the exterior world, progressing from one site to another with hard cuts between the seventy-eight scenes. So, while long shots and wide angles present the village and environs, the sudden shifts in location make it impossible to discern the lay of the land or to construct a mental map of the buildings' position relative to one another. For viewers, the overall result is a sensation of extreme constraint within the home, a lack of mobility outside, and a general sense of disorientation and dislocation. The framing and editing reveal that the long "era of peace" to which the narrator alludes has been anything but serene.

In this world on the cusp of war, temporal and natural thresholds proliferate, but the characters—and by extension viewers—are not invited to cross them. Adolescents on the verge of adulthood are not emancipated; death gives way to birth only to be met with death again; a whiff of bottom-up agitation emerges, although entrenched power structures squelch any rebellion.[17] The temporal in-betweenness, with the action transpiring from mid-1913 into mid-1914, is also translated into architectural aesthetics: the camera lingers in transitional spaces, often at windows or in doorways, at the bottom of stairs, in entryways, and under arches. When the pastor's children Klara and Martin are whipped for coming home late or the steward lashes his son (Enno Trebs), the camera waits in the hallway in the pastor's house or at the bottom of the staircase in the steward's home. The doctor's daughter, summoned to the casement window by her classmates, stands at a brink between interior and exterior, between allegiance to domesticity and the community of her cohort (fig. 2). Looking over her shoulder from the inner duskiness into the overpowering brightness, viewers are at a threshold, too, where the camera's lack of mobility amplifies the tenseness of the moment. It may pounce or zoom closer to the gaggle of children beyond the garden and picket fence—but it doesn't. The camera's location in dimly lit hallways, foyers, and near the grand entrance of the manor adds to our helplessness vis-à-vis the depicted events. What little

Fig. 2. The doctor's daughter Anna at the window. Collection Austrian Filmmuseum.

we are able to espy lies beyond our grasp. Furthermore, thresholds appear in the use of sound. The muffled screams of the pastor's son Martin being whipped behind the closed door underline our safe distance from the experience of physical pain. The disabled Karli's groans when he is discovered, beaten and bloodied, hover on the cusp of comprehensibility, but he cannot articulate the responsible party.[18] The film produces a sense of powerlessness as well as intellectual and emotional inaccessibility. Ultimately, intervention is impossible.

As stated, our awareness of what transpired after July 28, 1914 contrasts with the characters' lack of knowledge. In this bifocal view, Haneke's film recalls another *magnum opus* retrospectively assessing the era from the perspective of 1913: Robert Musil's novel *The Man without Qualities* (first published 1931). Haneke, who studied literature and philosophy at the University of Vienna, was approached in the 1980s to shoot Musil's magisterial fragment. While the director declined to adapt the unfinished work spanning nearly 2,000 pages, he incorporated the novel's paradoxicality and inversions into his 144-minute-long film. *The White Ribbon* presents the "good Germanic citizen" who enters the modern age unbeknownst to himself, small-mindedness intact. In the sixteenth chapter of Musil's novel, devoted to "a mysterious malady of the times," the protagonist Ulrich reflects on the era's tensions and the tipping point at which contemporary culture finds itself. The voice of the erudite narrator weaves in and out of the young man's consciousness:

> Had life in general reached a standstill? No, it had become more powerful! Were there more paralyzing contradictions than before? There could hardly be more! Had the past not known any absurdities? Heaps! Just between ourselves: people threw their support to the weak and ignored the strong; sometimes blockheads played leading roles while brilliant men played the part of eccentrics; the good Germanic citizen, untroubled by history's labor pains, which he dismissed as decadent and morbid excrescences, went on reading his family magazines and visited the crystal palaces and academies in vastly greater number than he did the avant-garde exhibitions.[19]

In *The White Ribbon*, the director situates his citizens in a peripheral space frozen in time; the agrarian community shares the conservative value system of earlier epochs. The characters in the film command positions in society that make them exemplars of their class by way of their profession: teacher, doctor, pastor, steward, landlord, shopkeeper. As Thomas Elsaesser has written in his study on *European Cinema and Continental Philosophy*, the men embody different aspects of the Enlightenment, lay-secularism (the teacher), Church authority (the pastor), as well as science and technology (the doctor).[20] With the exception of the teacher-narrator, all of them reject as pathological whatever does not fit into their worldview. The doctor harangues his mistress, the midwife, for her self-hatred. The baron scolds the tutor and the ailing baroness for the "menagerie" in the manor (he calls it a "monkey circus" or "Affenzirkus"). And the pastor rebukes the teacher for his "sick brain" when the latter articulates his suspicion of the children. They react like Musil's bourgeois, who "dismiss[es] as decadent and morbid excrescences" what he either does not comprehend or refuses to understand.

The White Ribbon explores the moment when certainty disappears in a time preceding upheaval. Absence becomes palpable in funereal, candle-lit spaces. Buzzing flies indicate decomposition and decay, their droning aurally augmented in post-production. Deaths and near-deaths pervade this society, and the doctor's son (Miljan Châtelain) is reprimanded for "ghosting" around (herum*geistern*). In this regard, Haneke also follows *The Man without Qualities*. Musil's eloquent narrator describes the changes in the atmosphere due to the general hollowing out of experience. Tautness gives way, and binaries lose their explanatory power:

> So what had been lost?
> Something imponderable. An omen. An illusion. As when a magnet releases iron filings and they fall in confusion again. As when a ball of string comes undone. As when a tension slackens. As when an orchestra begins to play out of tune. No details could be adduced that would not also have been possible before, but all the relationships had shifted a little. Ideas whose currency had once been lean grew fat. [...] Sharp boundaries everywhere became blurred and some new, indefinable ability to form alliances brought new people and new ideas to the top. Not that these people and ideas were bad, not at all; it was only that a little too much of the bad was mixed with the good, of error with truth, of accommodation with meaning. There even seemed to be a privileged proportion of this mixture that got furthest on in the world; just the right pinch of makeshift [*Surrogat*] to bring out the genius in genius and make talent look like a white hope, as a pinch of chicory, according to some people, brings out the right coffee flavor in coffee.[21]

The translators bring to the fore the implicit color scheme in their English version of *The Man without Qualities*, which fits nicely with Haneke's spectral whites and intense grey scale. While darkness predominates both literally and figuratively in *The White Ribbon*— the cinematographer has spoken of the low-lighting conditions on set—black and white cannot be conceived of as strict oppositions. The "blurred" boundaries and the emergence of evil from what was supposed to be good take the men in the film by surprise, and the extreme sharpness of the digitally enhanced images is pressed into the service of this blending.[22] The German word "Surrogat" has been translated in this paragraph as "makeshift," but it is closer to the English "substitute."[23] Musil's narrator, charting the changes in society, reflects on proxies and stand-ins within a fraying culture.

In *The White Ribbon*, the adolescent girls tread in their mothers' footsteps, and costuming emphasizes the continuities in women's lives beyond any familial ancestry or genetic predispositions. The adolescent girls in particular are caught between idealizing images of womanhood—note the neoclassical busts in the doctor's home and the manor, flanking the various female characters—and dismissive, patriarchal attitudes.[24] The camera that has just shown the doctor's daughter Anna in a long shot suddenly reveals the forty-year-old midwife Frau Wagner in a medium shot, with matching black dress and tight hair bun, in the exact position of the frame where Anna just was. The cut insinuates a temporal ellipsis, showing the girl "before" and the woman "after" as the same person. In turn, the pastor's daughter Klara comes into view at the end of the long traveling shot that began with the midwife's appearance. The tracking shot thus ends with another girl on the verge of adulthood. In this way, the montage of shots demonstrates the insidious transformation melding generations and cohorts (figs. 3a–c). The children's revolt follows the logic of substitution and allows strange admixtures to come to the fore. The docile Anna is equated with the strong-willed, but patiently suffering Frau Wagner (both are the doctor's sexual

Figs. 3a–3c. The logic of substitution.

victims), who stands in for the headstrong, subversive Klara. Klara—
alternatingly submissive and assertive—amalgamates elements from
both.

The opening sequences, which introduce this logic, also foreground
the literary model underpinning Haneke's undertaking. The white-
on-black title credit comes after credits naming the producers and
multiple funding agencies. "DAS WEISSE BAND" materializes in
Times New Roman capital letters. After a slight pause, the subtitle
"Eine deutsche Kindergeschichte" (A German Children's Story) is
slowly etched in white using an old-fashioned *Kurrent* script (fig.
4). The lack of background music is typical of Haneke's work, but in
this case the deliberate pace also activates us as readers, drawing our
eyes from left to right. In the German publishing world, the genre
(novel, drama, story) is routinely printed underneath the title on the
opening page. It guides prospective customers, but also inserts the
author in an illustrious lineage. Kraus's collage of scenes in *The Last
Days of Mankind* is characterized, for instance, as a Shakespearean or
Goethean "Tragedy in Five Acts with a Prologue and an Epilogue."
Musil's reflective first book of *The Man without Qualities*, avoiding

Fig. 4. Opening credits with subtitle in *Kurrent* script.

the designation "novel" altogether to assert its radical newness, is identified as "a kind of introduction." The *enfant terrible* of Austrian literature Thomas Bernhard, who influenced Haneke, also used such genre labeling in an unorthodox manner.[25] His novel *Cutting Timber* (*Holzfällen*, 1984) carries the subtitle "an agitation" or "arousal" (*Eine Erregung*), referring to Bernhard's penchant for exciting the public with his diatribes against complicity, obsequiousness, and opportunism. *The White Ribbon*'s subtitle, engraved on the screen, emphasizes the writing process and makes us wonder about the genre in Haneke's case. Are we supposed to read the image as we would the pages of a children's story, a "Kindergeschichte"? Should we think of this multi-part "tragic" story with narratorial prologue and epilogue as a "sort of introduction" to ideological indoctrination? Or is it an "agitation" for present-day viewers lulled into complacency about the ongoing threat of fascism? The careful left-to-right motion draws attention to the screen as a site of inscription, where the answers to the whodunit may be given.

In citing the paratextual conventions of written fiction, Haneke continues his interrogation of the way in which we are conditioned to accept mediated perspectives, plot lines, speaking positions, and narrative techniques as normal. In an effort to loosen the strictures of habituation, he questions the dominance of the visual over language but also the intellectual privilege often accorded writing over film. Haneke is not alone among directors articulating a suspicion towards images and visuality. The visual has generally been seen as untrustworthy in the European context since the 1960s as in the case of Haneke's avowed model Robert Bresson or the venerated Michelangelo Antonioni, as well as philosophers ranging from Jacques Derrida to Jean-François Lyotard.[26] However, in order to re-endow film with the ability to speak a kind of moral truth, Haneke needs the authenticating effect of literariness to re-endow the word with authority. The highly formal sentence structure in the dialogues, the absence of dialect (with the exception of the Bavarian

Sepp Bierbichler), and the lack of filler words such as "uh" and "um" when figures speak give the film a bookish quality. The high-cultural tone bleeds into the press kit, in which literary-sounding captions accompany the stills. A small sample suffices to provide the flavor: "What mischief are the children up to," "The pastor exhorts his son to candor," or "The baron despairs on account of the events" read some of the captions.[27] Particularly the final locution in German ("Der Baron verzweifelt ob der Geschehnisse") is a highfalutin indicator of the film's earnest literary style.

In the German-speaking world, a debate about historical factuality occurred concomitantly with the film's gestation during the 1990s.[28] The public discussion about fabrication in regards to the Holocaust, carried out in academic circles and highbrow media outlets after the publication of Binjamin Wilkomirski's highly problematic *Fragments: Memories of a Childhood 1939–1948* (1995),[29] is yet one more reason to be skeptical as soon as Haneke gestures towards facts, towards "honest" representation, as he does with the auratization of language at the outset of the film. The director wants us to reflect on how language bestows an aura on images, staking truth claims with an addendum such as "based on a true story" or, in Haneke's film, with the visual veneer of being historically accurate. In this regard, the opening sequence works on a metaphorical level: the wire strung across the misleadingly calm establishing shot trips up viewers from the outset. Thus the film begins with viewers' "Fall"—an entry into a postlapsarian state driven by the wish for knowledge and certitude, beyond falsehood and falsification.

The opening verbal chronicle, the narrator's effort to present itself as going on record, plays with the Biblical subtext I just evoked. The teacher's narration bestows sacredness on the accompanying visuals. "In the beginning was the Word [logos] and the Word was with God, and the Word was God"—John 1:1 underpins the film's tactical gambit at the outset. The story issuing forth from the Word is supposed to bring light into the darkness (cf. John 1:4–1:5). The narrator claims to be throwing an "illuminating light" (erhellendes Licht) on the past, enlivening it. The actor Ernst Jacobi (born 1933) intones the following lines after the credit sequence ends, but while the screen is still black:

> I don't know [weiß] if the story I want to tell you is true in all its details. Many things I only know [weiß] from hearsay, and after all these years I don't know [weiß] how to decipher some things, and many questions remain unanswered. But nonetheless I think I must recount the strange incidents that occurred in our village, because they may shed light on some of the events that happened in this country . . .[30]

In this case, the inherent boundaries of first-person perspective are reversed. With the homonym of "weiß" in "I know"/"Ich *weiß*" and the color white or "weiß," the narrator appropriates the lucidity of an all-seeing, all-knowing entity who can expunge the sins of the past—he can come clean and offer his version as a new beginning. As in Genesis, when God decrees "let there be light" (Gen. 1:3), the narrator makes visible. When he states that his story may "clarify" (from lat. *clarus*, meaning "clear," "bright," "luminous," "comprehensible," "evident," "gleaming"), light literally dawns on the plot's events and the black screen fades. We gradually see the field where the doctor rides along the central visual axis, moving from background to foreground. He comes into view in a wide-angle shot revealing the grasses, shrubs, and birch trees flanking the frame's borders—an Edenic place with few signs of human intervention (a wooden fence is off to one side).

However, the voice-over simultaneously establishes *and* disavows authority, evokes the Biblical logos *and* undermines the transcendent perspective. The narrator is endowed with God-like authority at the very instant when he stresses his limited perspective. After all, he anchors the narrative in the consciousness of a deeply human, limited psyche with his invocation of the first-person pronoun. The threefold mention of "weiß"—especially in negation—within the introductory speech draws attention to the way in which things escape knowledge; the repetition shows how the act of narration may have a whitewashing function. The narrator ultimately presents his relationship to the community as tenuous. He comes from a neighboring village and, as he admits at the end, he leaves after being conscripted into the army, never to return to Eichwald. As a result, he can profess a modicum of neutrality, but he also lacks complete access to the people who are the subject of his reflections.[31] From the voice's aged, gravelly texture, we surmise that the narrator has lived through World War I (he tells us so in the closing sequence) as well as World War II. As James Williams asks: "What actions, we may wonder, were committed by the narrator to ensure his own survival through two world wars up to the indeterminate present moment of his narration?"[32] Our doubt destabilizes the narrator's self-presentation as an unbiased observer. Furthermore, the horrible events he recounts are intertwined with his personal love story, which presumably skews his view. The rose-colored hues of first love are evident in some of the most tender scenes Haneke has ever filmed—the private concert in the schoolhouse by the warm glow of a petroleum lamp, the first dance at the harvest festival with its exuberant, swirling camera movement, the carriage ride through the lush landscape and chaste kiss (fig. 5). By comparison, the villagers' pettiness and cruelty are amplified, the teacher and his fiancée's virtuousness are underlined. The primary function of the narrator's framing activity, that is, separating the good (himself) from the bad (the villagers), is thus attenuated.

While the screenplay's language recalls nineteenth-century poetic realism or even the erudite locutions of Musil's modernist novel,[33] the insistent, self-reflexive frame has a more recent model. Haneke explicitly references the author Thomas Bernhard, whom I mentioned, in a synopsis of the film. In *The White Ribbon*, the filmmaker wants to "relativize reality" as Bernhard had in the

Fig. 5. The teacher and his fiancée Eva during their carriage ride.

novel *The Lime Works* (*Das Kalkwerk*, 1970).[34] The novel recounts previous violence from witnesses' conflicting perspectives. Reported speech—"Fro says," "as Wieser said," "as Konrad supposedly told Wieser," "according to Fro," and parentheticals inserted to indicate sources such as "(Wieser)" or "(Fro)"—produces a kind of *mise en abyme*, where it becomes impossible to tell who has said what to whom in the written transmission.[35] This technique stresses first-hand experience and gossip, hearsay and retelling; it highlights the interference when a message is communicated, despite efforts to keep the sources straight. The effect in Haneke, too, is a kind of parenthesis around a parenthesis around a parenthesis. The narrator's textured voice indicates a temporal caesura between the present moment of narration and the time period covered in the film. He draws attention to the loss accompanying any translation, be it from (imaginary) book to film or from one language to another (the intrusion of non-subtitled Polish in the original German version of *The White Ribbon* also emphasizes linguistic limitations, something the English release expunged with subtitles).[36] The vagaries of memory and the indeterminacy of rumormongering plague the retelling. As a story is conveyed from one person to the next, one historical context to another, loss invariably ensues and distortion comes into play.

Literal frames within individual images as well as obtrusive camera placement further highlight the perspectival aspect of knowledge acquisition. The careful compositions draw attention to distinct viewpoints and remind us to think about the sources responsible for imparting insights. The doorframes, windows, and gateways limit our visual and auditory access. Shots through architectural apertures are filmic equivalents to Bernhard's parentheses, attributing statements to characters in a dubious fashion. The informants become unclear in a reconstruction partially based on conjecture. Haneke's final storyboards bring to the fore the complexity of the camera's emplacement, as it navigates this slippery body of source material (fig. 6). Like the narrator himself, the camera shares news known via hearsay, and it often cannot transcend spatial boundaries. The camera's weird position outside the celebratory Christmas scene in the pastor's living room (fig. 7) and its surreptitious placement under the archway near the manor (fig. 8) stress its role as a transmitter of problematic information, where we wonder whose point of view this is. In such sequences, the camera is like an intrusive spy. It slinks around private spaces, not venturing in entirely, yet also not remaining at a safe distance. In the closing sequence, which I discuss at the end, the camera's perspective cannot be correlated with a human mind at all, but only with a transcendent viewpoint.

Inscriptions

The White Ribbon consistently thematizes the pressures of individuation in a society that operates according to patterns of abstraction and the goal of normativity. In this regard, let us return to the subtitle and the opening credits. The etching of the letters on the screen foreshadows

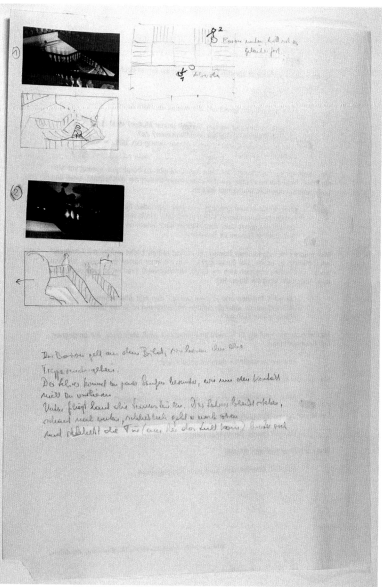

Fig. 6. Page from Haneke's script showing the camera's position in the stairwell. Collection Austrian Filmmuseum.

Fig. 7. Camera is positioned outside the room during the Christmas celebration.
Collection Austrian Filmmuseum.

Fig. 8. The camera as spy.

later moments of physical and mental inscription on the bodies and
psyches of the young. Haneke originally scribbled three potential
subtitles on the script from the 10th of April, 2008. As alternatives,
he noted: "The Story of the Teacher" (Die Erzählung des Lehrers),
"The School of Virtuousness" (Die Schule der Rechtschaffenheit),

"A Children's Story from Germany" (Eine Kindergeschichte aus Deutschland), and "A German Children's Story" (Eine deutsche Kindergeschichte).[37] By choosing the last variant, the film already introduces doubt, vagueness, and uncertainty—it undermines a subtitle's purpose. With the *genetivus subiectivus* and *genetivus obiectivus* of the composite noun "Kindergeschichte," we wonder whether this is a story of German children or a German story for children. Are they the subjects or the objects of this narrative? The indefinite pronoun "a" rather than "the" further complicates the generalizing impetus propelling any interpretation. How does this singular story stand in relation to other German children's stories? Is it one possible history (*Geschichte*) of German children? The question also arises: who is using this invisible stylus to write in cursive, in *Kurrent* script, across the black screen?

Handwriting marks the intersection of social and biopolitical concerns, as education produces middle class, bourgeois individuals as well as a people—the German *Volk*—in the course of the nineteenth century.[38] Script, taught in schools, is one means of integrating children into literate society. *Kurrent*, also known as German cursive, and its simplified variant *Sütterlin* (introduced in 1911 and propagated widely starting in 1935) only disappeared from schoolbooks in the first half of the 1940s. The *Kurrent* font thus acts as an authenticating effect. In 1913, this would have been the handwriting style children learned. However, the old-fashioned script in the credit sequence is illegible to anyone who is not of advanced age. Even the people involved in the film's production had to familiarize themselves with the now antiquated German cursive: some advertising posters contained an incorrect double "h" in "deutsch" as well as in "Kindergeschichte" (fig. 9). The slowly unfurling script, in a style most viewers are unable to read, focalizes attention on the subtitle's limited comprehensibility.[39]

Haneke first utilized this technique in the credits of his appropriately named *Code inconnu* (*Code Unknown*, 2000). In *Code*

Fig. 9. Draft of poster for French release, Le Ruban blanc.
© Christian Blondel / Les Quatres Lunes, 2009.

inconnu, there are often prosaic impediments to comprehension, which go beyond being ignorant of a particular tongue. While the letters of the alphabet may be the basis of a common language, we cannot always unlock their meaning for material reasons.[40] For instance, *Code inconnu*'s credit sequence appears in miniscule capital sans serif letters on a black background. In *The White Ribbon*'s credits, we oscillate between legibility and illegibility, between comprehensibility and incomprehensibility, even after the *Kurrent* script has disappeared. The credits for camera, sound, editing, scenery, costume design, music, etc. fade in and out in tiny Times New Roman font, as do the words "A Film by MICHAEL HANEKE." The auteur's name is displayed ambivalently, capitalized but miniaturized and hence obfuscated. We are meant to read but come up against obstacles. We are supposed to bear witness to scenes of inscription, but the presentation sometimes does not allow us to be reliable eyewitnesses. As if warning us about making overhasty judgments, the lettering calls attention to the limits of—and limitations on—visibility as well as the complexity of becoming "readers" capable of adjudicating moral responsibility.

The film establishes an additional tension between a person's handwriting and the codified letters of the printed alphabet, between individuality and standardization. As Carlo Ginzburg has argued, the movement toward a scientific paradigm and modern society begins with the reproducibility of texts, with the elision of personal textual markers such as voice or handwriting.[41] The flawless penmanship unfurling in the opening credits is not that of a child—or, for that matter, of a human being at all. The perfect writing recalls Haneke's 2005 film *Caché* (*Hidden*), which begins with computerized letters appearing in neat rows from left to right until they fill the screen. The unspooling words create friction between the realm of the digital, in which the main character Georges (Daniel Auteuil) works, and the analog realm, which records the victims' *cri de coeur* in the form of drawings, analog photocopies, and videocassette tapes. For instance,

a few reproduced postcards, which are based on crude crayon
sketches, depict a head spitting up blood. Like these photocopied
drawings in *Caché*, the cursive in *The White Ribbon* belongs both to
the realm of standardized, reproducible perfection as well as to the
individualized analog realm, which relies on originals. On the one
hand, it gestures beyond individuality, toward mechanical and then
digital reproducibility with total standardization. On the other, the
Kurrent script conjures up authenticity, originality, and singularity.
The young people in *The White Ribbon* try to negotiate these
conflicting poles as they rebel against the normative constraints of a
society educating and indoctrinating them. Contemporary viewers
are caught in a similar position, as they watch the high-definition
digital work comment on the analog history of edification.

Black Pedagogy

If the *Kurrent* penmanship intimates the personalized gesture within
an abstracted system of writing and thinking, it also indicates the
larger educational structures that attempted to produce similar (even
uniform) individuals beholden to certain moral codes and models of
development. In the film, Haneke examines educational institutions
and methods of child-rearing belonging to a long Western tradition
that was thoroughly criticized in post-1968 Germany. In doing
so, he makes direct use of the aforementioned work of the critic
Katharina Rutschky (1941–2010). In 1977 Rutschky, part of
the generation invested in unmasking authoritarian practices in
everyday life, published her book *Schwarze Pädagogik: Quellen zur
Naturgeschichte der bürgerlichen Erziehung* (Black Pedagogy: Sources
for the Natural History of Bourgeois Education), a compendium
of eighteenth-, nineteenth-, and twentieth-century texts on
"Erziehung," the difficult-to-translate noun meaning schooling,
child-rearing, upbringing, disciplining, formation. Employing the

caustic designation "black pedagogy" in her title, Rutschky reveals the pernicious side of Enlightenment pedagogy with her polemically chosen excerpts from various treatises espousing reform. These include works by famed pedagogues Campe, Basedow, and Pestalozzi, psychological studies, serial novels, handbooks, and manuals. Taking her cue from Norbert Elias's magisterial *On the Process of Civilization* (1939, republished 1969) and Philippe Ariès's *Centuries of Childhood: A Social History of Family Life* (1960), Rutschky demonstrates how emotional and ideological continuities in *Erziehung* continue well beyond the "pedagogical century," the name given the eighteenth century with its Rousseauian inclinations and efforts to make pedagogy a public rather than a private matter. Historical drawings in her six-hundred-page compendium show strange devices to improve posture, architecture for teacher-centered instruction (*Frontalunterricht*), and climbing equipment to strengthen and discipline young bodies. In Rutschky's view, the discovery of the child within the family unit goes hand in hand with efforts to internalize authority and subjugate children under duplicitous pretenses. She impugns viewing childhood as an incubation period, for it facilitates the concept that teachers need "total access" (*Zugriff*) to the child. The youngster becomes a "blank space, a tabula rasa, which every pedagogue desires in order to more easily inscribe himself on it."[42] Such a system propagates itself, churning out more pedagogues who reproduce the institutions that have created them. Child-rearing and disciplining practices (*Erziehung*) first supplement and then displace education (*Bildung*), which is interested more in the transmission of knowledge and the full unfolding of an individual's capacities.

Like Rutschky, Haneke emphasizes "*Erziehung* as total institution" in order to reflect on the afterlife of the antiauthoritarian, antiestablishment West German discourse in the 1960s and the 1970s.[43] Left-leaning student protesters and others campaigned against the status quo and what they considered political psychopathology, authoritarian personality structures, and the continuities with the National Socialist past.[44] The intellectual and cultural climate of this period deeply influenced the director, who was working at the regional German public broadcasting corporation Südwestfunk in Baden-Baden in the late 1960s as dramaturg and script reader. He came into contact with the militant left, including Red Army Faction co-founder Ulrike Meinhof, as he himself has remarked.[45] As Roy Grundmann has also demonstrated, Haneke is deeply beholden to Theodor W. Adorno's sociopolitical commitment during this period.[46] Adorno's radio dialogues on *Erziehung* between 1959 and 1969 influence the film's engagement with an upbringing that leads to militant proclivities. Adorno's popular radio programs and talks, published posthumously as *Erziehung zur Mündigkeit* (Raised to Maturity, 1970), cover many theoretical and practical issues, from the inability to work through the Nazi past to the problems facing teachers. For readers of the collected essays and transcribed dialogues, a clear line connects "The Meaning of Working through the Past" (Was bedeutet: Aufarbeitung der Vergangenheit) from 1959, "Taboos on the Teaching Vocation" (Tabus über dem Lehrberuf), broadcast in August 1965, and the best-known essay "Education After Auschwitz" (Erziehung nach Auschwitz) from 1966; a red thread runs through these pieces and "Education for Debarbarization" (Erziehung zur Entbarbarisierung) of 1968 and the separately published essay, "On the Question: What is German" (Auf die Frage: Was ist deutsch) from 1969.[47] Rutschky's compendium also exerted an extraordinary influence in the late 1970s due to the work of the psychoanalyst Alice Miller. Miller based her book *For Your Own Good* (*Am Anfang war Erziehung*, 1980) on Rutschky's *Black Pedagogy*. *For Your Own Good*, with the word *Erziehung* in the German title, is an exploration of the regulation of drives, as well as the internalization of bourgeois norms of acceptable and deviant behavior. Miller uses case studies, including that of Adolf Hitler, to illustrate the deleterious consequences of the kind of pedagogy shown in *The White Ribbon*.[48] All in all, the period in the wake of

National Socialism is also a "pedagogical half-century," intensely invested in what antiauthoritarian instruction might look like.

The topic of pedagogical practices already comes in the first sequence. The doctor's dressage lesson, as Haneke notes in his synopsis, is emblematic of efforts at *Erziehung*, training people to be fully "functional" adults.[49] In the second sequence, when Klara is introduced at the end of the long take, she explicitly apologizes for her brother Martin's impolite behavior employing the term "Erziehung." Klara's lexical choice, used in conversation with the midwife, actually sounds quite jarring to a native speaker of German. We expect her to apologize for his manners, but not the way in which he was raised *tout court*: "Excuse us, Frau Wagner [. . .]. We are so worried, you know. That's why Martin forgot how he was raised" (seine *Erziehung* vergessen).[50] Martin has not been trained successfully, in Klara's estimation, to conform internally and externally to society's mores. In *The White Ribbon*, many pedagogues mold children like Martin: the house tutor, nursemaids, midwife, parents, teacher—who admonishes children, but is never seen imparting factual knowledge or critical thinking skills—but most importantly the pastor. Indeed, the minister is the pivotal "black pedagogue." In tight two-shots and shot/reverse shot scenes with angled cameras, we see and hear him "inscribing" his faith-based tenets on the minds and bodies of children. He often dominates the frame, towering over a child or standing in the bright light, while the child tilts his or her head upward or is indistinctly visible in the background (fig. 10). When the pastor berates his daughter in front of her schoolmates, Klara—whom the pastor has pulled by the ear (!) from the front to the back of the classroom—is shown from a distance, regardless of her positioning within the room. The camera allies itself with the clergyman, looking over his shoulder while he prays the "Our Father." It moves ever closer to his face as he talks about his efforts to "form" the children into "responsible human beings." As the "spiritual leader" (geistige *Führer*), the Protes-

Fig. 10. The domineering pastor.

tant clergyman has shaped his daughter with a "white ribbon . . . to help her evade sin, selfishness, envy, impurity, lying, and sloth."

Haneke's white ribbons thus clearly relate to Rutschky's black pedagogy: he incorporates parts of the texts she selected into his dialogues, as in the classroom scene just described. The screenplay's compression of Rutschky's already condensed excerpts further stresses the excessive nature of "enlightened" punishments under the guise of parental love. Haneke takes up a stratagem that modernists like Karl Kraus pioneered. In doing violence to texts by taking them out of context and collaging them in new constellations, the director and screenwriter makes visible, clarifies, and reveals overarching patterns.[51] For example, the pastor's lecture explaining the white ribbon in Klara's hair is taken from J. Heusinger's five-volume text, *Die Familie Wertheim* (The Wertheim Family, 1800–1809). In Rutschky's abridged variant, she gives the Heusinger excerpt the polemical subheading "How the Vice of Lying is to be Treated" to underline the supposedly "curative" properties of pedagogical interventions. Bad behavior is imagined as an illness to be healed; in *The White Ribbon* the pastor becomes a medic of the soul.[52] His advice to Martin about masturbation is a similar intervention. The warning about onanism comes from J. B. Basedow and J. H. Campe's collection *Sammlung einiger Erziehungsschriften* (Collection of Some Pedagogical Writings) of 1778, also excerpted in Rutschky.[53] Finally, the pastor's reflections on the pain punishment causes parents subscribe to the ideas outlined in an instructional manual from 1887, which Rutschky entitles "Pedagogical Blows are the Blows of a Lover": "The father punishes his child, and he himself feels the blow [...] If the father is a proper paternal teacher [ein rechter *Schulvater*], he also knows how to love with the cane if need be."[54] Reproductions of therapeutic contraptions in Rutschky's book, like the child with the harness for good posture, call to mind Martin's immobilization for masturbating in his attic room.[55] To sum up: the most insidious aspects of child-rearing through the centuries are made evident through the pastor, whose pontifications collate ideas from an entire history of pedagogical reform. His speeches fuse the various linguistic styles from multiple epochs, adding to the film's temporal iridescence—the late eighteenth-century sounds different than the late nineteenth in terms of semantics and sentence structure. Although the narrated time is 1913–14, the pastor sometimes speaks as if he were in 1778 or 1809.

Visual ties in the film proliferate to demonstrate the ubiquity of a pedagogical practice literalizing the "ziehen" (pulling) and "Zucht" (cultivation, discipline, breeding) in the German word Er-*zieh*-ung. Ideological ties bind this community together, and the group demands ever more ligatures to maintain the authoritarian status quo. People are bound in subtle and unsubtle ways by things used to fasten, secure, hold in place, affix, mark, and threaten. There is the wire, the pastor's clerical collar, the riding crop, the string with the warning message around the injured Karli's neck, the rope with which the tenant farmer hangs himself, the garlands in the church, the white sliver of snow-covered ground. Ribbons, of course, adorn the hair and sleeve of the pastor's children in public and the son's wrists in private. The steward's daughter Erna (Janina Fautz) crochets white bands that fall chastely onto her lap, which is all the more jarring as she is discussing a murder attempt on her infant brother. From these physical ties we invariably make an associative leap to the traces they leave: the impression on the birch bark from the trip wire (the doctor looks down, offscreen, at this mark), the white gauze band across Karli's eyes, the striae that whips leave on the children's skin, the tenets engraved on the children's hearts.

Haneke inserts his filmic "ribbon" into the semantic chains *The White Ribbon* evokes. In one advertisement in the Austrian Film Museum's archive, the film is represented as an elongated filmstrip with the resplendent white landscape extinguishing distinct features. The digital film, wrapping itself in the guise of the analog, recalls the technological ties to the past, on the level of history and media history. The film ribbon compels us to look and want to break free. *The White Ribbon* punishes viewers for the sake of educating them. The filmmaker, like the pastor, follows a moral imperative: he secures these images in our minds in the name of consciousness-raising. All along, he shows how intergenerational inscriptions create a double bind. The rigid moral compass that adults instill in children in the name of an ethicopolitical and religious order as well as the older generation's inability to conform to the self-same order put the children in an impossible situation. In their case, violence begets violence, and for every tie that is broken, another one comes about. The film leaves us to ponder whether there is any "outside" to the dialectic *The White Ribbon* outlines.

Working Through Working Through

Haneke links the subcutaneous violence in all social strata present in 1913 to the rise of fascism a decade onward, the upsurge of the Red Army Faction fifty years later, and the spread of terrorism forty years after that. Michael Rothberg's book *Multidirectional Memory: Remembering the Holocaust in the Age of Decolonization* (2009) helps us understand this melding of epochs.[56] Rothberg explains how various groups' histories of victimization come into conflict in the public sphere. In some of the acrimonious debates he describes, one group's history is seen to displace other histories. In this scenario, the "public sphere in which collective memories are articulated is a scarce resource" in which "the interaction of different collective memories [. . .] takes the form of a zero-sum struggle for preeminence." Against this view of memory as a finite entity where one past elides another, Rothberg argues that memory is an encompassing thing in a state of continual negotiation and re-negotiation. He examines the period between 1945 and 1962, which witnessed the "rise of consciousness of the Holocaust as an unprecedented form of modern genocide and the coming to national consciousness and political independence of many of the subjects of European colonialism."[57] Rothberg's reflections provide context for multidirectional memory in Haneke's oeuvre, where an awareness of the Shoah's centrality co-exists with the cognizance of other oppression. The competitive struggles over recognition that continue to "haunt contemporary, pluralistic societies" animate Haneke's films, where "displacement and substitution in acts of remembrance" characterize figures' response to historical and social injustices.[58]

In many ways, Haneke also follows Adorno and Max Horkheimer's *Dialectic of Enlightenment* (1947), to which Adorno alludes in his essays on *Erziehung*.[59] For Adorno and Horkheimer, writing against the backdrop of National Socialism and the collapse of the liberal state, the Enlightenment project reverts to the superstition and myth out of which reason supposedly emerged. The so-called historical progress of reason turns out to be a return to barbarism. The domination of the external world can only be had at the expense of subjugating one's inner nature and through a pathological relationship to the body. The film invokes this German tradition of working through the past in a psychoanalytically and sociologically inflected vein. As Jennifer Kapczynski has written, viewers interpret *The White Ribbon* foremost as a film about the rise of National Socialism, with a view to the failure of reason that Adorno and Horkheimer outline.[60] The name of the village, after all, is a composite of Obersturmbannführer Adolf Eichmann and the concentration camp Buchenwald.[61] The narrator, compelled to recount, assigns a therapeutic function to his telling, which psychoanalysis ascribes to the act of narrating the past.[62]

In the film, we are also faced with what Michel Foucault in the 1970s called the "repressive hypothesis." The avid policing of sexuality is part and parcel of the bourgeoisie's rise and its manner of exerting pervasive power. Haneke changed the socioeconomic status of his pastor and reduced the number of impoverished tenant farmers working the estate in his final screenplay.[63] Instead of a priest who runs a small guesthouse to augment his modest salary and a slew of poor day laborers, as Haneke originally envisioned, the finished film presents a well-to-do clergyman in prosperous surroundings and a lascivious steward with a spacious home. The film thereby becomes a tale of the middle class, its hang-ups with the body, and its reliance on the nuclear family as the fundamental unit of society. *The White Ribbon* illustrates how sexual repression—in the middle class—brings with it the infinite proliferation of discourses on what sex is, how it is to be regulated, and who is to engage in it. The pastor, the doctor, the baron, and the teacher all talk about sexual behavior or physical needs in scene after scene, and they are keen on preserving the outward semblance of honorable sexual relations to maintain their power. The pastor wants to prevent masturbation; the doctor only confesses his strong sex drive to his lover but conceals his molestation of the daughter; the teacher promises not to impregnate his fiancée and "disgrace" her. The German aristocracy does not indulge in the promiscuity historically associated with the French court. Instead, the baron reprimands his wife about her Italian lover like any bourgeois husband would. He is only concerned with whether or not she actually slept with her suitor. He does not really care if she loves the successful banker from Lombardy.

In this regard, too, *The White Ribbon* might be seen as part of Haneke's ongoing interest in countercultural tenets of the 1960s, including how National Socialism persists in gender relations. As Dagmar Herzog has written, the initial post-1945 period witnessed an avid discussion about licentiousness, with both Protestant and Catholic churches in West Germany espousing chastity as a way of overcoming the National Socialist period and its perceived debauchery. The left of the 1960s, Herzog maintains, jettisoned earlier interpretations of Nazism as prurient, instead espousing the belief in sexual liberation as a means of overcoming lingering fascist tendencies.[64] Until *The White Ribbon*, Haneke was more cautious than 1960s liberal intellectuals and leftist activists who equated sexual repression with Nazism or Christianity. His films such as *Lemmings* (*Lemminge*, 1979) or *Caché*, which both deal with the generation that comes of age in the 1950s and 1960s, tend not to draw a causal relationship. However, an early synopsis of *The White Ribbon* makes a direct connection between a "morality perverted long ago" and the "disposition toward fascist emotionality."[65]

Women's Meta-Commentary

Returning to the complexities of perverted moral codes and latent fascist tendencies also gives Haneke the opportunity to continue the gender legacy of New German Cinema (NGC). It, too, offered sociopolitical criticism in the form of literary adaptations, with complex female characters like Rainer Werner Fassbinder's 1974 *Effi Briest* or Volker Schlöndorff's heroine in *Coup de grâce* (1976). Figures like Maria Braun (*The Marriage of Maria Braun*, dir. R. W. Fassbinder, 1979) or Katharina Blum (*The Lost Honor of Katharina Blum*, dir. Margarethe von Trotta and Volker Schlöndorff, 1977) point out the semantic difference between loving and liking someone, between making love and fornicating. Haneke, too, has often portrayed free-thinking women who can parse the differences between love and lust. However, he explicitly made his television film *Fraulein: A German Melodrama* (*Fraulein—Ein deutsches Melodram*, 1986) to refute what he perceived as the hypocrisy of Fassbinder's *Maria Braun*. In his view, women are less capable of re-invention than men—they have more completely internalized society's restrictions, even if they are more critical toward them. Like Maria Braun, Katharina Blum, or Johanna (Angelica Domröse) in *Fraulein*, the women in *The White Ribbon* distinguish between copulation for sex's sake and out of love—and this irrespective of their social class, so whether baroness or midwife. But in keeping with Haneke's views of limited gender mobility, the baroness does not desert her husband and the midwife stays with the abusive doctor.[66] Haneke also has drawn attention to the fact that the women of the Red Army Faction, a recurrent subject in NGC films such as *Germany in Autumn* (dir. Alexander Kluge et al., 1978) or *Marianne and Juliane* (*Die bleierne Zeit*, dir. Margarethe von Trotta, 1981), were an inspiration for figures like Klara. Ulrike Meinhof and her film *Bambule* (1970), about pedagogical practices aimed at wayward girls, are also an important source. Finally, Meinhof's Christian background as well as her RAF comrade Gudrun Ensslin's Protestant upbringing play into the presentation of the young women and their revolt against the fathers in *The White Ribbon*.[67]

In the film, the baroness Marie-Louise provides the most cogent metareflections on the sociohistorical milieu and its gender politics. She is set apart from the villagers through her perspicacity and emotional intelligence. Marie-Louise is introduced via sound, like the narrator. We hear disembodied piano playing accompanied by a less accomplished flute—mid-stream, the flutist hits a wrong note. Immediately thereafter, we see the baroness through the eyes of her son Sigi, whose attention has been concentrated on the dead horse in the yard and the torchlight of the men discussing it. As he pivots, with his viewpoint connecting the outside world and the inside realm, Sigi draws attention to his mother's role as a mediator between Eichwald and the surroundings. The baroness at this moment is playing Schubert's variations on "Withered Flowers" for piano and flute in E minor, D. 802 (*Trockne Blumen* in the original German, published only in 1850, well after Schubert's death). The house tutor apologizes for the wrong note that causes the duet to break off. In his words, he is not Fredrick the Great (1712–86). Marie-Louise remarks that the Prussian king would hardly have been playing Schubert (1797–1828) and asks the tutor to take up the variation again and concentrate. In a few terse sentences, she draws attention to the mixing of temporalities and the attention this interweaving requires of viewers. *Caveat spectator*.

In this segment, we are also made aware of the film's permutation principle: *The White Ribbon* masterfully composes variations on a single theme. The perpetuation of violence takes the form of child against adult, adult against child, adult against adult, child against child. Like the baroness's piano playing at a speed too quick for the tutor's liking, the narrative presents many kinds of malevolence with extreme rapidity. Within the embedded story, the pace is a steady forward movement, although interruptions occur. In this sequence with the house tutor, the baroness's piano playing is twice disrupted, first by a wrong note, then by the intrusion of her son. She wants her "field of vision," or "Blickfeld," cleared of distractions, and she demands that young Sigi remove himself.[68] In a larger sense, we are forced to think about our field of vision throughout the film. We try to separate the important information from the red herrings, the visual and narrative distractions within each frame. What clutters our *Blickfeld* and interrupts our concentration? Her words, delivered with vehemence, refocus our attention on the macabre décor from which the sound bridge distracted us. The opulent floral arrangements befit a burial; the lugubrious lighting evokes a funeral ceremony; the theatrical drapery transforms the interior into a proscenium for youth's final curtain call (note how Sigi is about to enter onto the stage when his mother chastises him). The emanation of music from offscreen space should also bring to mind Wilhelm Müller's lyrics for the Schubert song cycle, alerting us to the changing seasons and the lyrical self's mourning of unrequited love.[69]

The baroness's positioning at the piano alerts us to women's place within this society: they are caught between conventional image repertoires of romanticized femininity and the real world of devalued female existence. Marie-Louise is seated facing the tutor, who is standing and dominates the space with his phallic flute. Designer Christoph Kanter's careful mise-en-scène underlines this movement between sentimentalized idealization and humiliating disparagement. A white marble bust in the background links the baroness to the doctor's daughter, who appeared a few segments earlier with a similar neoclassical statuette behind her in profile (figs. 11a–b). The statues symbolize a disembodied feminine ideal for all classes, which the women's lived experiences perpetually contradict. The cool, smooth marble and pallid plaster cast contrast with women's debased bodies, especially in the lower class. In the segment with the corpse of the tenant farmer's wife, we only see her exposed genitals and naked legs in the impoverished bedroom where the body is being washed before the wake. The doctor deprecates the midwife's flaccid skin and bad breath, comparing coitus with her to mounting a horse.

The location choices in *The White Ribbon* accentuate the psycho-sexual dynamics and visualize psychoanalytically inflected theories of working through the past. In this regard, Klaus Theweleit's influential account of gendered fantasies and self-constitution around World War I deserves mention. Theweleit drew attention to the psychic economy of the 1920s right-wing White Terror in the former Eastern parts of the German Empire, the area where *The White Ribbon* is set (Haneke briefly considered Poland and the Czech Republic, before moving to towns in the former German

Figs. 11a–b. Neoclassical busts flank the baroness and the doctor's daughter.

Democratic Republic, 200km northwest of Berlin). For Theweleit, soldiers' fears of feminine subversion led to both imagined and enacted violence against the stigmatized female body—and other bodies perceived as effeminate. Theweleit's 1977–78 dissertation *Male Fantasies*, printed with the revolutionary publishing house Roter Stern, quickly sold thousands of copies and garnered reviews in left-leaning publications as well as mainstream newspapers.[70] The popularity of Theweleit's argument—that an internalized, everyday fascism lurked in relations between men and women—also owes much to the book's appearance at the height of the leftist German terrorist movement of the 1970s, with its prominent female guerrilla fighters, self-lacerating betrayals, and autocratic power struggles.[71]

Some archival photos offer further clues to Haneke and his costume designer Moidele Bickel's representation of the baroness, who is trapped by conflicting gender perceptions. In the director's screenplay now held in the Austrian Film Museum, a small photocopy of a black-and-white image is affixed to a page, glued directly below the hand-drawn storyboard: it shows a cluster of white-clad ladies in front of a mansion (fig. 12). A handful of gentlemen in dark suits flank the women on both sides of the imposing stairway, with gaps separating the men from one another and the group as a whole.

Fig. 12. Historical photo of aristocratic family. Collection Austrian Filmmuseum.

Children are congregated in the center. The multigenerational family is draped photogenically across the stone staircase, along which white flowers bloom. Like the women in the photo, the baroness is dressed entirely in white during the harvest festival. In the later dinner scene with her husband, when the fraught discussion about infidelity ensues, she wears a resplendent white blouse—it provides a stark contrast to the serving-woman's dark hues and the women's dour clothes generally. However, rather than placing the baroness in a group, as is the case with the ladies in the historically sourced image, Haneke often isolates her in the frame and in the story itself. While an extended family portrait inspires the film's costuming and setting, the film reduces the conflict to the nuclear family. This is typical for Haneke's scenarios, which are often centered on a father-mother-child triangle.

Indeed, his storyboard choreographs groups versus individuals, with the latter being the focal point of the village's suspicion or ire—and the audience's interest. People are artfully assembled and set in opposition to each other. This makes for arresting visuals and enables viewers to ascertain who is in control. We see this staging in Haneke's rough sketch above the photocopy of the large family (fig. 13). In his diagram, the villagers have congregated at the foot of the manor stairs during the harvest festival, providing a sea of heads onto which the aristocrats gaze. The sketch attributes the point-of-view shot to the baron ("POV Baron") alone, the master-of-all-he-surveys. The baroness partakes of this heightened perspective, but she is physically subordinated to her husband and visually crowded by the pastor and her son, both dressed in black (fig. 14). In another metafilmic moment, she talks to the teacher immediately thereafter about the missing "chorus" (*Festchor*) during the thanksgiving feast—a subtle reminder of the chorus's function in Greek tragedy, where it comments on the main action. While the teacher blames the pastor for the lack of such a communal response, the clergyman is insidiously perched between the two speakers (fig. 15). Once again,

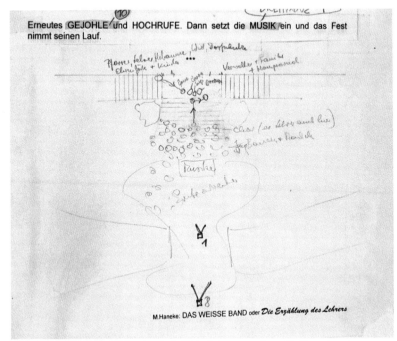

Fig. 13. Haneke's storyboard showing the individuals (pastor, teacher, midwife, etc.) vs. the group (musicians, harvest workers) at the harvest feast. Collection Austrian Filmmuseum.

the baroness, stunningly beautiful from the front and softly backlit, remains powerless and is visually ostracized—an exquisite outlier. Despite her acuity and greater empathy, she is incapable of asserting herself and prompting change. She alone has to make up for the collective rejoinder that the story lacks.

During the dinner scene, in which things come to a head between her and the baron, the camera looks down at her as tears well up and she explains her need to get away. After her husband has ordered her to remain in the room and she has taken her seat, the camera sequesters her in the frame. Significantly, she is not shown in a two-shot with her husband in this sequence. Their son Sigi has been attacked a second time, nearly drowned because the steward's jealous

Fig. 14. The baroness "caught" between the men.

Fig. 15. The baroness and the teacher.

son coveted the youngster's pretty fife. The simple flute brings us full circle to the opening, when the baroness was introduced with the tutor-flautist. At this late juncture, she may well be giving voice to viewers' exasperation with the unceasing cruelty that has transpired: "But I can't stand it here. Less for my sake [...] I am leaving this

place because I do not want Sigi and later the twins to grow up
in an environment dominated by malice, envy, apathy, and brutality.
The story with Sigi's little fife was the final straw. I have had enough
of the abuse, threats, and perverse acts of revenge."[72] She implies
that the law of the talion—an eye for an eye, a tooth for a tooth—
is restricted to the village. Given her special status within the film,
these words raise the issue of scalability. What is the relationship
between Eichwald's crimes and the surrounding world? If her
earlier assertion about Schubert and Frederick the Great cautioned
viewers to be aware of historical telescoping and its implications
for multidirectional memory, this speech warns about overhasty
generalizations in moving from microcosm to macrocosm.

Germanness

At stake in Haneke's undertaking is nothing less than an elucidation
of what it might mean to be German in the modern period. This
brings us back to the model character of Haneke's film. While
Haneke commented in an early sketch that he did not want to create
a treatise (*Abhandlung*) about the predisposition of the populace
toward fascism, it is hard to avoid this impression.[73] Not only do
exemplary figures represent their professions and social classes, but
foreshortened scenes limit understanding of different personalities
and abrogate emotional investment. With the exceptions of the
pastor's small son Gustl (Thibault Serie) and the doctor's youngster
Rudi (Miljan Chatelain), even the children remain rather schematic.
The film comes across as an abstract reflection on the internalization
of power, the performance of authority, and the suppression of others
in the name of perverted ideals.

In his early synopsis, Haneke describes an "Ordnungssystem"—
meaning both a "system of order" and an "ordering system"—underpinning the children's behavior. "I would like to show," he writes, "a

group of young people who, situated in a seemingly secure [*festgefügt*] system of order, make the principles of this order absolute in their childish idealism; in this way they become the guardians of these ideals and therefore judges over those who fail in front of them, and thus they demonstrate in an exemplary fashion the complete perversion of those very ideals."[74] A syllogistic logic reigns in this firmly joined world: "He has the power who is instituted as the stronger thanks to (performed) authority [*(Spiel-)Autorität*]. He who has power must be obeyed. He who does not obey is bad. He who is bad must be punished."[75] The children in the film operate according to these unquestioned premises and unleash chain reactions (if a, then b). The children witness the performance of authority but also play (*spielen*) at being authoritative and authoritarian. They inadvertently uphold the system that subordinates them because they do not question the grounds on which it is based. Not only are they unable to distinguish between game and reality, the totalizing nature of the system does not reveal a gap (it is "festgefügt") where they can assert their autonomy. They perpetuate the corrupted Christian ideals that employ brutality as a deterrent, retrospectively justifying their own punishment in the name of that closed system.

Paradoxically, the film evokes the "Germanness" of these thought structures through scrupulous attention to peripheral detail, in the service of which architectural historians, folklorists, and musicologists were consulted.[76] Haneke and his assistant director researched the architectonic details of farm buildings, churches, manor houses, mills, stables, and barns in the Brandenburg region. The crew was interested in secular as well as religious habits. They looked into the minutiae of schooling: were boys and girls mixed in single classrooms, and when would they have had vacation? Was the seating order done according to age or gender? What kind of accoutrements would have been in a classroom, what materials available to students? Would children really have kissed their parents' hands before going to bed, as they do in the scene with the pastor and his wife? (fig. 16) How would

Fig. 16. Children kiss their parents' hands as part of the good-night ritual.
Collection Austrian Filmmuseum.

the coffin of someone who committed suicide have been carried? Were women and men separated during mass? How were bread and wine administered during confirmation? Music specialists from Berlin, Leipzig, and Freiburg, listed as contacts, were presumably consulted on some questions regarding the harvest scene. The team's correspondence suggests that they also asked regional specialists with degrees in military history and musical ethnology. The crew wanted to find out how many musicians would have been at such a festive gathering. What kind of music would there have been in 1913? One expert suggested that the orchestra at the thanksgiving festival include brass instruments (none were incorporated) and another that they would have played popular songs as well as military music— and we do hear a flourish with wind instruments before violin and clarinets play a waltz. Other queries were directed at military historians. Would the volunteers for the army (*Landwehr*) have attended church in uniform in August 1914, as Germany mobilized for war (in the film, we see the recruits with flowers pinned to their lapels)? Finally, the scene involving the destruction of the cabbage

Fig. 17. The peasant's son Karl destroys the cabbage harvest. Collection Austrian Filmmuseum.

patch necessitated the advice of a botanist (fig. 17). When do these vegetables ripen and would that work out with the film's chronology? That is, could the custom of taking revenge on a miserly manor lord by destroying the cabbage harvest—which Haneke transforms into a striking allegory of death with scythe—actually have occurred at the harvest feast?

In sum, the fetishistic attention to period reconstruction provides another answer to the question "What is German?," a query Adorno had posed nearly fifty years earlier.[77] Haneke's answer required historical research *and* philosophical abstraction. *The White Ribbon* uses both historicity and ahistoricism to elicit the multidirectional memory that moves back in time *and* forward to the present. The precision of the costumes, buildings, and customs reconciles us with the plot's *Modellcharakter*, and the composite locations do gel into a coherent site. The shoot took place not only in Netzow, Mark Brandenburg, but also in Söllenthin, Michaelisbruch, Zechlinerhütte, Schloss Johannstorf/Dassow, and a studio in Leipzig.[78] While we may not be able to chart the distance between the doctor's house and the manor, the steward's home and the pond, we nevertheless get a sense of a sequestered space, surrounded by fields and forest. In an effort to circumscribe the mentality that made possible the rise of ideological extremism, Haneke tries a two-pronged tactic: a schematic model with itemized detail.

In examining what it means to be German, Haneke's film draws on famous precedents. He inserts himself into the tradition of photographers like August Sander (1876–1964) and philosopher-critics like Adorno (1903–69) or Walter Benjamin (1892–1940). Sander's photographs, an openly acknowledged source of inspiration, begin in the late Wilhelmine period and transition into the Weimar Republic and the Third Reich. Sander attempted a catalogue of representative types in his magnum opus *People of the Twentieth Century: A Cultural Work of Photographs Divided into Seven Groups*, which remained unpublished at the time of the photographer's death in 1964. The multi-volume work—over 600 portraits arranged into portfolios first brought out in 2002—presents a survey of urban and rural society in the service of "absolute fidelity to nature," according to the photographer.[79] Sander's images are grouped according to professions and milieus: "The Farmer," "The Skilled Tradesman," "The Woman," "Classes and Professionals," "The Artists," "The City," and "The Last People." In 1929, Sander published an excerpt with the title *Face of Our Time: Sixty Portraits of Twentieth-Century Germans*.[80]

In literature, Walter Benjamin's annotated collection of letters by well-known writers, philosophers, and politicians entitled *German Men and Women* (*Deutsche Menschen*), accomplished a similar re-evaluation of what it might mean to be German in the early twentieth-century. Benjamin's collection, first printed in installments in the daily newspaper *Frankfurter Zeitung* from 1931–32, was brought out in book form under a Christian pseudonym after the Nazi takeover in 1936. The twenty-five letters from Kant, Lessing, Goethe, Brentano, Büchner and others have generally been seen as repudiating Nazi conceptions of greatness. The poetic dedication at the beginning of the book serves as an affective digest: "Honor without fame, / Greatness without splendor, / Dignity without recompense."[81] Benjamin's short commentaries, interspersed between the letters, stress the writers' sadness but also their calm assessments; notable is the stoicism with which the reverberations of war are borne in private life. Like Sander, Benjamin excavates another Germany, capturing the bourgeoisie in historical moments of crisis. Benjamin's conceptualization of the project likewise included a division into groups, with sections devoted to "School and Life," "The Decline and the Founding of the Reich," and "New Viewpoints."[82] He, too, suggests alternative avenues for conceiving of oneself and one's compatriots, far removed from chauvinist, hegemonic terms.

With the waning of the Cold War order and twenty years after Germany's reunification, the question "What is German?" has not lost its resonance. Indeed, in a time of increasing nationalism and xenophobia as well as supranational convergence with the European Union, Adorno's self-reflexive question, Benjamin's alternative genealogy, and Sander's probing catalogue provide Haneke with an intellectual lineage. In particular, Haneke has often described his herculean search for faces that would be redolent of Sander's portraits, auditioning more than 7,000 children.[83] *The White Ribbon* continues this interrupted aesthetic history of portrait photography in the post-1945 period, where landscape and architectural photographers (Bernd and Hilla Becher, Andreas Gursky, Candida Höfer, Thomas Struth, Thomas Demand) dominate public perception.

In the scene when the pastor scolds Klara and Martin for having coming home late, the camera lingers on the siblings' faces with downcast eyes. The twitches in their facial muscles register their terror when the pastor announces that the youthful offenders will be strictly punished. We move around the oval table from close-up to close-up, noting the children's unusual traits, the girls' firm plaits and the boys' long lashes, the freckles and the serious mouths. Similarly, during the long shot at the tenant farmer's kitchen table—

the numerous offspring are seated for a frugal repast—the camera hangs back to take in the children's upturned visages. Adult faces, too, receive individualized treatment. A series of six portrait photos appears during the baron's address to the church congregants (figs. 18a–f). In close-up, we study the faces in slow sequence: three men without proper collars, seemingly poorer farmers, then four women, one of whom is the steward's wife. Each person's face is crisply photographed. Only their surroundings are somewhat blurred.

In Döblin's foreword "Of Faces, Images, and Their Truth" accompanying Sander's *Face of Our Time*, the writer lauds the photographer's attempt to get beyond simplistic conceptions of mimetic verisimilitude. The celebrated modernist writer extolled the photos'

Figs. 18a–f. Portraits of the congregants.

representative nature. Sander's portraits are not interested in capturing what Döblin calls commonplace similarity (*Ähnlichkeit*). Instead, they seek out "universals" (*Universalien*), surpassing particular human beings. In estranging what has become too familiar, Sander achieves an "expansion of our visual field" (*Erweiterung des Gesichtsfeldes*). The scientific thrust of the photographer's work, Döblin argues, lies in presenting a study of a society in complete flux. Sander's photographs make visible the "rapid change in moral beliefs" at the beginning of the twentieth century. Döblin's example of the pastor is pertinent to our context. In Sander's image "Protestant Clergyman, 1928" (*Evangelischer Geistlicher*, 1928), Döblin notes a diremption in the faces' expressive coherence as a group: the "Protestant clergyman, a superlative image, his pupils [*Zöglinge*, from *ziehen*] surround him, but they already have faces that don't fit their teacher's expression and his cassock" (fig. 19). Different time frames and experiential dimensions register within a single photo, as the hardened expressions of the younger generation contrast with their teacher's kindly if somewhat benighted smile.

This is one side of Haneke's undertaking: like Sander, the director becomes a cultural historian and a "comparative anatomist."[84] The camera, trained on faces, transcends the individual quality of each person to measure societal developments that lay the groundwork for ideological extremism. In German historiography of the 1960s and 1970s, for instance, some social historians focused on the petit bourgeoisie and the capitalists' role in the rise of National Socialist ideology during the Weimar period. Similarly, Haneke's montages demonstrate the socioeconomic explanatory power of portraits when they are grouped together; the photo series provide a counterweight to the domineering role of single patriarchs like the pastor. Looking at the different clothing of the churchgoers, we are sensitized to different economic strata within the small town. We note the emotional variance of the reactions, running the gamut from alert, bemused, enthralled to pensive or smug, and we ponder whether the

Fig. 19. August Sander, "Protestant Clergyman, 1928." © Die Photographische Sammlung / SK Stiftung Kultur–August Sander Archiv, Cologne / ARS, New York.

different affective registers are due to the distance an individual may have from power (i.e., the baron).

In the end, however, the film swerves away from its tendency toward typological or sociological abstraction, recalling the individuals who make up Eichwald. Haneke stresses the moment of self-alienation via representation that facilitates critical analysis. Döblin also writes the following about Sander's portraits: "Suddenly we become strangers to ourselves and have learned something about us. It is extremely good to learn something about oneself." With humor, the writer suggests that portraits help individuals realize how they misconstrue their independence from others. Rather than seeing conditions for what they are, namely as limits on personal autonomy, people tend to bask in deceptive notions of individual self-presence and self-knowledge. In this way, Sander's images allow an "expansion of our field of vision," moving beyond aesthetic photographers' search for specious originality or "nominalistic" photographers' desire for cheap particularity.[85]

Thus the film limits its comparative anatomy via portraiture, tending instead to concentrate on the psychoanalytically inflected moment of individual self-estrangement and self-knowledge in (mis-) recognition. The news of Archduke Franz Ferdinand's assassination follows a marital dispute and the *paterfamilias'* harangue about infidelity, rather than coming after a communal event. There is only one doctor, one nobleman, one pastor, and one midwife in this one-horse town, and the camera lingers on their faces at length. These people do not engage in colloquy with their counterparts outside of Eichwald. No letters reach them, no telegraph or telephone line connects them to other members of their class in stratified Prussian society. Haneke's research notes never once mention contemporaneous means of communication, by which residents in such a small border town would have been in touch with an empire beyond their purview. The telegraph became a fixture of everyday life by the 1870s, telephones more common after 1900—

but neither touches Eichwald in 1913. Significantly, only women like the baroness and the teacher's fiancée Eva (Leonie Benesch) bring news of the outside world, and the bicycle is a rare means of modern transport linking Eichwald to neighboring towns. We are left to wonder how the news from Sarajevo reaches the steward, with nary a newspaper or telegraph pole in sight. Only messages conveyed by word-of-mouth travel quickly. Rumors move "in Windeseile," at the speed of wind, as the teacher states. Only these provincial, parochial sounds perforate the walls and forbidding façades. Once again, we need to be skeptical of the film's generalizing drive and its *Modellcharakter*.

Two montage sequences of landscape images further displace the diagnostic force of the photo series from human universals onto the environment. When the teacher's aged voice breaks the linear continuity of the embedded story to remind us that horrible acts took place during the time of his budding courtship, the open landscape enters as a force in its own right. The flatland rekindles memories of post-1960s films that programmatically distanced themselves from the sublime mountain scenery in affirmative 1920s *Bergfilme* (mountain films) and 1950s *Heimatfilme* (homeland films).[86] However, Eichwald's unspectacular topography of terror calls to mind the "open countryside" or "platte[s] Land," where Adorno claimed that de-barbarization after 1945 had been less successful than in urban areas.[87] Static shots of the village and its environs accompany the teacher's voice-over when he talks about the good weather at the end of the year.[88] The snow's luminosity was blinding: "[. . .] it hurt the eyes. We all did not suspect that this would be the last turn of the year in peace." The camera withdraws from the immediate environment shot by shot, moving from snow-covered village to niveous field. Intense light fills the screen, with only a sliver of snowy ground and two trees (one in leaf!) visible in a panoramic shot (figs. 20a–c). The white ribbon of land makes us wary, as do the leaves. Viewers have learned to distrust the positive connotations

Figs. 20a–c. Eichwald in winter.

accompanying whiteness in a film that undermines traditional color associations: when white is foregrounded, visibility is limited and the eyes cannot discern distinctions.[89] The resolution to the mysterious events is no closer in the glaring light.

Three images of the landscape occur when the teacher reflects on the year's end; five long shots of the environment are shown toward the film's close, after the news about possible war spreads through Eichwald and before the midwife announces that she will go to the police with information on the culprits. In the second, closing bracket, the camera suddenly peers at Eichwald from a distance. Located in the forest, it looks out at the village (fig. 21). Then the camera shows the village recumbent in the full sun, with its church tower from a different angle. Gone are the thick tree trunks that partially hindered our view. Finally, the camera is immersed in the thriving wheat, but no village is to be seen. In three long shots, we only get the wheat fields. In the final image the sky dominates over the terra firma, with the two miniscule trees on the screen left (now they really are full of leaves). Gone from our field of vision is the small town in which the rumor mill grinds away.[90] Who is doing the looking here? When the

Fig. 21 The camera peers at Eichwald from the forest.

Fig. 22. Peasant farmers harvesting. Collection Austrian Filmmuseum.

camera presents the ripe fields in the sunshine, the harvest festival comes to mind. While the bounty matures, we imagine the scythes being sharpened to reap what has been sown. This time there will be a harvest of men, as there had been one of crops (fig. 22). A photo series taped into Haneke's screenplay emphasizes the importance of these landscape images: the montage sequences of pseudo-stills act as the visual equivalent of a bracket, cordoning off events and further quarantining Eichwald (fig. 23).

The landscape series thus undermines the film's topographical and historicizing impulse, its effort to evoke a localizable northern German town at a specific temporal juncture. The landscape shots remove us from human time and place us in the natural rotation of the seasons. What about people's culpability now? If the first montage produced a tension between the teacher's limited perspective and authorial/god-like omniscience (with the landscape becoming Haneke's own white ribbon), the second montage asks us to ponder the coming world war and its aftermath from nature's perspective. Nature is indifferent to the fate of human beings, their accidents, murders, beatings, and maltreatment. The gruesome man-made

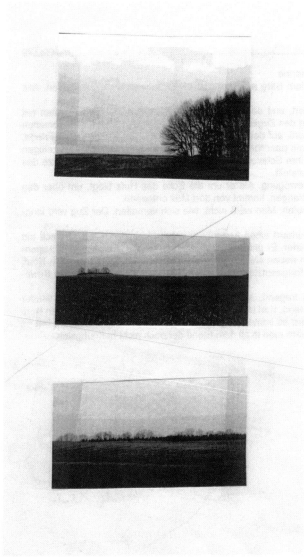

Fig. 23. Three landscape photos in Haneke's script.
Collection Austrian Filmmuseum.

events merging into war happen in a microscopic place within an infinitesimally small temporal span—without relevance to a larger organic cycle that is truly global and everlasting

An Ecology of Images

The White Ribbon interrogates the conditions for its own possibility as a feature film about violence—to do so, it looks at the status of the individual image. Although some reviewers stress the gulf separating *The White Ribbon*'s stylistic opulence from the aesthetic austerity of Haneke's other theatrical features set in the contemporary world, the director actually stages his dramatic departure as a concerted return. Haneke's engagement with the medium of photography in *The White Ribbon* can be traced back to his television film *Three Paths to the Lake* (1976), based on Ingeborg Bachmann's eponymous story from 1972. The protagonist's successful career as a photojournalist is subjected to scrutiny—the voice-over narrator (Axel Corti), the lover Franz Josef Trotta (Walter Schmidinger), and the protagonist Elisabeth Matrei (Ursula Schult) herself question photojournalism's purpose.[91] "Why do you take pictures?," Trotta asks Elisabeth accusingly, "Do you think you have to photograph [*abfotografieren*] destroyed villages or corpses for me to be able to imagine war?" A jarring montage sequence of photographers vying for the perfect shot reveal the rapacious, commercial logic driving them (fig. 24). Trotta's deprecatory locution—"abfotografieren" instead of the more common "fotografieren"—emphasizes the sterile aspect of photography, which simply *re*-produces and facilely *re*-presents. Its creativity lies, perhaps, in its introduction of error or falsehood, akin to the circulating rumors in *The White Ribbon*. Individual photos are never guarantors of some greater truth. Photos undermine what happens on the soundtrack in *Three Paths*: while a photomontage shows Arthur Miller and Marilyn Monroe, the

Fig. 24. The competition for the perfect shot.

voice-over narration mentions Churchill and Hemingway. Other photos the photojournalist has supposedly taken include her in the frame. Haneke's TV film compels us to imagine a different image practice beyond the one we observe here. *Three Paths* demands that we, like Elisabeth, think about the reason for images, especially those depicting suffering and violence. The film asks us to think about why they proliferate and whether their avowed ethical impulse is disingenuous. As I mentioned earlier, Haneke writes himself into a tradition of filmic modernists skeptical of the building blocks of cinema, calling into question the tools of his craft.

Trotta articulates what Susan Sontag called an "ecology of images" in her 1973 book *On Photography*, published nearly concurrently with Haneke's Bachmann adaptation. Writing about an analog historical moment, Sontag underlined the "force" of photographs, which "comes from their being material realities in their own right, richly informative deposits left in the wake of whatever emitted them, potent means for turning the tables on reality." Precisely because photographs are an "unlimited resource, one that cannot be exhausted by consumerist waste," she writes, people should apply a "conservationist remedy" to their use.[92] When Sontag returned to her analysis with a quarter-century's distance in *Regarding the Pain of Others* (2003)—as Haneke did with his reprise of *Three Paths to the Lake* in *Code inconnu* (2000)[93]—she defended her earlier analysis. Writing in 2003, Sontag denied that images leave no position outside permanent mediation from which they could be criticized. Like the fictional Trotta, Sontag argues that the "specificity of the photographs' accusations will fade; the denunciation of a particular conflict and attribution of specific crimes will become a denunciation of human cruelty, human savagery as such" (122). Unlike Trotta in *Three Paths to the Lake*, Sontag does not detect cynicism in the diffusion of such images. Trotta speaks of "malice," "impertinence," "indignity," "dumb arrogance," and a deep-seated hypocrisy in those who disseminate such pictures to raise awareness.

Haneke's films could be seen as taking Trotta at his word—*re*-presenting pain out of moral outrage is perfidious. He calls attention to the various visual and auditory components that come together to make us suffer with the characters on screen. He queries how the registers for depicting violence change over time: the perception of verisimilitude in suffering—how real an experience feels to viewers—is a product of the state of film technology at any given moment. The inflationary use of represented violence, especially in the era of the digital, requires particular vigilance, something works like *Benny's Video*, *Funny Games* (1997), or *Caché* already made clear. However, although historical juxtapositions inevitably sacrifice nuance and encourage comparisons,[94] multidirectional memory is inevitable. This also aligns with Sontag's 2003 views "regarding the pain of others": war photography and photos of suffering invariably change viewers' experiences of pain. While victims may feel it is intolerable to have their "sufferings twinned with anybody else's," as Sontag contends, it is nonetheless important to allow "atrocious images to haunt us." This spectrality may be more effective than asking people to "never forget."[95]

The White Ribbon ultimately validates such an alternative image practice. The landscape series in the film are poignant counter-cinematic moments, pressing artificiality into the service of "artifactuality," as Haneke puts it.[96] The photomontages remind us of the original building blocks of cinema and reflect back on the mediated nature of Haneke's own pedagogy.[97] In the first montage of the winter landscape, the snow was added in post-production as one of approximately seventy digital enhancements.[98] These images measure the distance we have traversed since August Sander and his photomechanical era. *The White Ribbon*'s exceeding brightness, into which the characters are released, is only possible in an era of extremely light-sensitive cameras and digitalization. The perfection and hyperrealism of the images draw attention to the act of visualization itself; they insert a pause in the unfolding action and allow critical reflection. While the inky darkness and grayscale convey a somber mood in low lighting,[99] the brightness outdoors brings to the fore the atmosphere of chilling epistemological blindness: knowledge hurts. The young girl Erna, a "seeress" (*Hellseherin*), and the disabled boy Karli, his eyesight damaged, reveal the dialectic of blindness and insight in the film. The weakest become those most able to discriminate between guilt and innocence, and their percipience comes about when they are least able to see—at night, in dreams, when their eyes are injured. Finally, the whiteness in the photomontages recalls the materiality underpinning the cinematic experience, which makes possible the interrogation of Enlightenment pedagogy in the first place: an empty screen as today's variant of a white canvas for a landscape painting, a blank page for a novelistic undertaking, or photo paper for developing a portrait. Haneke inscribes his story on this white space, beckoning toward a utopian world in which *The White Ribbon* would not be necessary as a morality tale.

The Unresolved Mystery

Although the film gives no clear-cut solution to the crimes, the culprits can be discerned by way of strict symmetries and careful perspectival lines. At the beginning, the doctor rides into the frame from the exact midpoint, a small speck growing larger. After his sudden fall, a cut again turns our attention to the central vanishing point—from which his daughter emerges. The wrongdoers are often caught in this manner, in a *mise-en-abyme* staging. They are in the foreground of the image plane, centered and in plain sight. The mirroring quality—with one perpetrator reflected in the other—underlines the infinite regress of culpability in a world where such social structures and psychic economies predominate. Numerous guilty parties exist across generations.

The director's studied open-endedness, his strong desire *not* to offer narrative closure, is counteracted on a formal level in this way. Other Haneke films such as *Code Unknown*, *Caché*, or *Happy End* (2017) stress their lack of resolution, the viewers' inability to judge, and the situations' indecipherability. Yet the filmmaker has always encouraged us to move our eyes along sight lines, into and out of the central vanishing point or horizontally across the picture plane in a side-to-side motion. He has done this to question our desire for depth, with all its attendant metaphorical accretions of interiority, soulfulness, and truthfulness. For a film like *The White Ribbon*, which emphasizes reading and writing, the horizontal movement is especially important. The answer lies where the axes intersect at the front of the image plane.

It is helpful to think back to an early adaptation of Haneke's as a statement of visual intent: *Wer war Edgar Allan?* (*Who Was Edgar*

Allan?, 1984) is another open-ended mystery. The TV film is, like
Three Paths to the Lake, far more traditional in its stylistic means
than Haneke's theatrical releases, but it contains many elements we
could consider trademark. Visual clues lead the student protagonist
(Paulus Manker) on a fruitless pursuit down dark Venetian alleys and
through cavernous interior spaces with a strong central vanishing
point. The fugitive is a secretive older man, aptly named Edgar Allan
(Rolf Hoppe). As he drops hints about drug trafficking and murder,
he keeps the youthful protagonist in suspense. The young student
scans the recesses of space while trailing Allan. In the course of the
chase, the student breaks the fourth wall and reflects out loud on the
vexed relationship between hidden, latent meanings and manifest
clues scattered on the surface, between sanity and madness. Like
Edgar Allan Poe, who in "The Purloined Letter" (1844) draws
the detective's interest toward the answer lying on the surface, the
person of interest in *Who Was Edgar Allan?* leads us to the front of
the televisual image.[100] At the end of the eighty-minute-long film,
a dolly back moves viewers away from the wanted poster revealing
Edgar Allan in black outline. Swirling snowflakes fill the frame. The
young protagonist enters, pauses to study the poster, then walks from
the background to the foreground along the central axis, exiting the
frame down the middle. Viewers are left to ponder the intersection of
horizontal and vertical axes and the dance of black-on-white "snow,"
the TV noise preventing us from catching the culpable person(s). The
flurries continue, and another zoom outward brings into view the
television screen on which we watched events unfold. Viewers are
reminded of the film's "flatness" and the story's hypermediation. From
the wanted poster to the close-ups of television screens, surfaces for
inscription abound, which both facilitate comprehension and obscure
legibility. In another scene, the student and Edgar Allan are seated
next to each other on a banquette in a storied Venetian café, Caffè
Florian. The careful architectonic symmetry emphasizes the men's
similarity to one another, but it also draws attention to the mirror

behind them with its bottomless complexity and infinite regression, Haneke builds on this spatial tension to reflect on our desire for (tele)visual depth. We hope we can dig deeply enough, eliminating the interceding media. Were we able to move into Renaissance space beyond the screen's boundaries, we believe we would finally enter into the promise of (non)representation. However, we only have the media surface with its many scintillating effects.

The White Ribbon, carrying our eye from back to front (with the doctor and Anna) in scene 1 and then from left to right along the foreground (with the midwife and Klara) in scene 2, keeps bringing us to the front of the image and makes the sign of the cross over the entire story. In no other film has Haneke's interest in Christian symbolism and ritual melded so distinctly with his formal proclivities and distinctive mystery-structure. Klara, as the instigator, is associated with the cross.[101] When she apologizes for her brother, she stands underneath the timber frame of the school building—a cross-like shape. After her father drags her to the back of the classroom, she remains near a row of coat hooks, producing another cross with her body. In retribution for her public humiliation at school, she crucifies her father's songbird. Of all the youngsters, she most often commands the central position in the middle of the frame. As the children withdraw from the discussion with the midwife, Klara is flanked on each side by two girls (fig. 25). When the pastor scolds his daughter for being the "main actor" (*Hauptakteur*) in an "abject play" (*erbärmliches Schauspiel*),[102] she is in the exact midpoint of the image until she suddenly drops out of the field of vision with a fainting spell. When the teacher discovers her peering into the midwife's home, she is again in the middle of the picture. She is nearly in the center of the image when the teacher questions her and Martin about the events in the village. In short, she appears where the horizontal and vertical axes intersect, moving into and out of deep space and standing in the midpoint of the frame in crucial scenes.

Fig. 25. Klara's central position. Collection Austrian Filmmuseum.

By placing Klara centermost and motivating her actions with reference to the Protestant faith, Haneke continues one strain of thought about the Red Army Faction mentioned earlier. Some observers link an internalized Protestant moral code and 1970s terrorist radicalism, especially in the case of the female members of the first generation of terrorists. Gudrun Ensslin's father was a Protestant minister; Meinhof came from a religious family in Hamburg that was close to the anti-fascist Protestant church.[103] The problems are not solely between fathers and sons locked in oedipal conflict, an element the steward introduces when he comments obscenely on his infant son suckling at the mother's breast. In *The White Ribbon*, fathers and daughters are at odds, too. As was the case with the mirroring situation between the culpable doctor and Anna, the pastor appears immediately after the teacher's interrogation of Klara. The white doorway frames the clergyman—he is equidistant from its sides. His home with its theatrical aspects, where heavy curtains emphasize the proscenium arch, provides the stage on which he and others perform (fig. 26). He is also a "main actor" in

Fig. 26. In the pastor's theatrical home.

this "abject play," an accusation he leveled against his child. Guilt is concretized visually and then refracted endlessly in a dizzying mirror effect.

The film dialogue further underlines the historical link to the Red Army Faction. The RAF's language of defiance against the status quo is brought in by way of Klara's formulaic responses. Klaus Theweleit analyzed the leftists' language of the 1960s and 1970s in an influential lecture published in *Ghosts* (1998), where he looks back on his own revolutionary fervor during the 1960s.[104] To reject the "parental terror" (*Elternterror*) and the "still-Nazi parents" (*Immer-noch-Nazi-*Parents), the student opposition incorporated psychoanalysis, Marxism, American rock, and internationalism into its lingo, but at the same time replicated the authoritarian "soundtrack." Theweleit discusses the conditioning (*Dressur*) of the RAF prisoners, whose "training during early and late childhood, school years, streams out of every pore of the[ir] letters." They copy their parents' "regulations, prescriptions, directives, accusations, appeals/roll calls."[105] The RAF's language became increasingly rote in the course of the 1970s, and Klara's phrases in *The White Ribbon* are formulaic. When asked why she did something, she responds: we were worried, we wanted to see if we could do something, we wanted to help (scenes 3, 4, 64, 73). "Helping" is never meaningfully defined. In what way could children help when such catastrophes have befallen people? Reference is attenuated, and the victim dematerialized.

Klara's name—derived from *clarus*, ergo *illuminating*—points to the visual and auditory issues bedeviling the community. The Latin term is, as I learned from the comparative literature scholar John Hamilton, not only linked to visuality, but also to acoustics and audibility. *Clarus* is related to many terms reaching back to the Indo-European root *kel-, klā-*, as in Latin *clamor* ("loud cry, shout"), *calare* ("to call together, summon"), and *classis* ("a summoned social class"). *Clarus* describes a strident sound, an outcry, a clamor, the clarion's alarm. In German, Klara may suggest visual or conceptual "clarity," but she is not "klar" in any purely logical sense. She cannot explain (*erklären*), resolve, or enlighten (*aufklären*). In Haneke's original synopsis, this leading part was Anna's, who convinces others "softly" and "assertively."[106] In the character's iteration as Klara, she is paradoxically incapable of producing a well-defined sound that could stake a truth claim—compare her garbled screams in the classroom. Instead of an aurally comprehensible and intelligible discourse, Klara speaks unclearly. Her internalization of parental authority and her externalization of authoritarian rule also come together when she determines who speaks. She seizes the word whenever children confront adults, but only with her standardized, empty answers. She forbids her brother from making statements and the other children from talking to the police. Theweleit's statement about the RAF— "[a]s if the ghost of the parental generation, which they had wanted to escape, had slipped back into them in an inverted exorcism"[107]— applies perfectly to this tow-headed young lady who handles her teacher's damning indictment of her with complete sang-froid.

The abstracting principle underwriting the film's sacrificial rituals is a quotation from the Bible—"For I the LORD your God am a jealous God, visiting the iniquity of the fathers on the children to the third and the fourth generation." Exodus 20:5 is written on the paper tied around Karli's neck when he is found in the woods, in the same *Kurrent* script as the film's title credits. The inscription on the paper leaves out the next verse, which promises a God capable of showering affection. The jealous god, who punishes those who hate him, shows "steadfast love to thousands of those who love me and keep my commandments." In the omission of Exodus 20:6, Haneke continues his ongoing interrogation of societal *froideur* and justifies his own violence against the spectator.[108] Adorno describes the coldness that made Auschwitz possible as a fundamental lack of love in the essay "Education after Auschwitz." Love is difficult, if not impossible, in contemporary capitalist life, and Adorno acknowledges that love cannot be mandated, especially since the adults who need to show it to their children are products of a loveless society. For him, "[l]ove is something immediate and in essence contradicts mediated relationships." For Adorno—and Haneke in the philosopher's wake—love cannot be summoned up in "professionally mediated" relationships such as those between teacher and student. Western society, where everyone "pursues their own interests against the interests of everyone else," is unable to produce conditions where an exhortation to love would be anything other than an oppressive injunction or an idealistic platitude. In "Education after Auschwitz," Adorno illuminates the subjective dimension of social coldness. The philosopher thereby seeks to counteract ideological extremism of all types and provide the groundwork for a "political instruction [...] centered upon the idea that Auschwitz should never happen again."[109] In this regard, Haneke is his most astute pupil.

Coda

When the film closes, the first-person frame is flouted: a transcendent perspective replaces the human one. The point of view does not

Fig. 27. The final tableau in the festive church. Collection Austrian Filmmuseum.

coincide with the teacher's, who has been our guide and instructor. *The White Ribbon* ends with a long shot of the church interior, as the children's chorus begins to sing (fig. 27). The teacher positions himself to the left of the choir at the top of the tableau. He directs Martin Luther's hymn "A Mighty Fortress is Our God." The lyrics stress the spatial dimensions of unwavering faith, envisioning belief as a secure military fortress. "A mighty fortress [Ein' feste Burg] is our God, / A bulwark never failing: / Our helper He, amid the flood / Of mortal ills prevailing," sing the children, with a professional choir acoustically overlaying their voices.[110]

In closing, the narrator re-articulates the lack of knowledge he had thematized at the beginning. But before he does so, his language plays on the "hardiness" and "festiveness" inherent in the word "fest" mentioned in the children's chorale (*ein' feste Burg*). The sense of enclosure, whereby home is imagined as a fortification (*Festung*), conflicts with the joyous festival (*Fest*) and centripetal force of impending change. The fortress has long been breached metaphorically, and for viewers the scene becomes a proleptic funerary mass.[111] Before the final fade-out, the narrator describes the general excitement:

> The whole town came to the festive service on the following Sunday. An atmosphere of expectation and departure lay in the air. Everything would now change. In light of the anticipated war, Eva's father had retrieved his daughter from the city and, due to her incessant pleas, come to Eichwald in order to see the home and workplace of his future son-in-law. With a view to perhaps soon being able to call the beloved being my wife, this day was a feast day for me as well.

> [Zum festlichen Gottesdienst am folgenden Sonntag kam das ganze Dorf. Eine Stimmung von Erwartung und Aufbruch lag in der Luft. Alles würde nun anders werden. Evas Vater hatte seine Tochter angesichts des zu erwartenden Krieges aus der Stadt nach Hause zurückgeholt und war nun, auf ihr inständiges Bitten, nach Eichwald gekommen, um Heim und Wirkungsstätte seines künftigen Schwiegersohns in Augenschein zu nehmen. Mit der Aussicht, das geliebte Wesen möglicherweise schon bald meine Frau nennen zu dürfen, war dieser Tag auch für mich ein Festtag.]

Visibility has been at issue throughout, and there is no reason to believe that the teacher's prospective father-in-law will be able to have a closer look (*in Augenschein nehmen*). Nor, perhaps, will the narrator's prospects (*Aussicht*) come to anything. The teacher's sense of breaking open (*aufbrechen*) the fortress Eichwald is certainly different from the community's sense of departure (*Aufbruch*) with the outbreak of war. The celebratory atmosphere (*festlich, Festtag*) with the young volunteers for the war effort in the first row and the garlands strung across the balcony conflicts with the negative particles strewn throughout the narrator's closing speech: not only did the pastor never again (*nie wieder*) mention their acrimonious discussion, he never (*niemals*) made good on his threat to have the teacher fired. Instead, the teacher was recruited into the army and never saw any of Eichwald's inhabitants again (*niemand*). The triad of never again (*nie wieder*), never (*niemals*), and no one (*niemand*) accentuates the war's temporal break and its finality. The optimism is built on shaky foundations.

As the final image shades to gray and then black, we mull the teacher's power to shed light on events (his "illuminating light"), in contrast to the pastor's intimation that he would denounce the teacher to the authorities. The pastor had threatened to "blacken" (*anschwärzen*) the teacher's reputation if the pedagogue told the police he suspected the children. The frame in this scene highlights the conflict between the representatives of church authority and Enlightenment reason. The pastor emerges from the central axis into the foreground, while the strong horizontal lines lead our eyes to peruse the front of the picture plane. The vertical wooden pillars contrast with the garland's left-to-right stringing and the horizontals of the gallery. The white painted wood concretizes the tension between change and stasis (fig. 28). An impossible light source brightens the windows on both sides of the church simultaneously.[112] In the same way as the script in the title credit writes itself horizontally, emanating in a disembodied manner from both nowhere and everywhere, we "read" the final frame like a page. We scan from left to right, seeking clues as to what the preceding two hours may have meant in regards to interpreting the past and imagining a potential future. We might think we are witnessing the upending of the stratified societal order, where the pastor has been relegated to an inferior position, the baron disappears screen left, and the young soldiers move to the forefront. However, the picture plane, with its clear top and bottom, still determines the social order. The figures remain caught in coordinates over which they have little to no control. An aesthetic solution—strategic containment—has been found to the plot's irresolution. The teacher's emplacement in the

Fig. 28. Tension that the architecture creates is visible in Haneke's storyboard.

background, separated from the villagers, highlights the problematic nature of his articulations. He is positioned aloft and off-center. He speaks from the present about a past in which he was somehow complicit but from which he tried to stay aloof.

Since this scene visually echoes an earlier scene in the church, viewers are forced to reflect on the ending's point of view. In the

Fig. 29. The baron speaking in the church.

earlier sequence in the church, the baron warned that the inner peace of Eichwald would be lost were the guilty party not discovered (fig. 29). In Haneke's storyboard, the baron speaks before the assembled. He is seen from the perspective of the believers in the back of the nave, and a thickly drawn cross in the center dwarfs him. In the closing two-minute-long segment, the camera is positioned in the sanctuary, behind the altar—it approximates the cross's placement. The camera looks down from a slightly raised vantage point onto the people convened before it. Perhaps human will is severely limited after all, and the worldly allies of church authority are as powerless as the teacher. An entity whose existence exceeds the film's framework has preordained the story's outcome.

The phrase "never again," a leitmotif for the postwar West German Federal Republic mindful of its Nazi past, implicitly echoes through the narrator's last statement during the fade to black. The generality of the post-1945 slogan precludes the exact attribution of blame, as culpability becomes diffuse. We are left to wonder whether a period film that emphasizes the difficulty of apportioning responsibility is capable of raising historical awareness. Haneke's literary and stylistic framing of the events certainly helps contain the explosive argument the film is subtly making—namely that clear attributions of guilt or innocence become impossible across time and mediated histories. While reviewers were largely positive about the film on both sides of the Atlantic, a few US American critics cast doubt on *The White Ribbon*'s ability to elucidate the conditions it seeks to understand. A. O. Scott, writing for the *New York Times*, complained that the film "mystif[ies] the historical phenomenon [Nazism] it purports to investigate. [...] 'The White Ribbon' is a whodunit that offers a philosophically and aesthetically unsatisfying answer: everyone. Which is also to say: no one."[113] In restoring some of the historical background, I hope to have demonstrated that the film's indictment is indeed more specific, reaching back into the eighteenth century.[114] Ways of rearing children particular to the European Enlightenment made German systems of hypocrisy, collusion, and oppression possible across generations. These systems arose from the heart of the middle-class nuclear family to take aim at that very institution.

CREDITS

Director:
Michael Haneke

Writer:
Michael Haneke

Production Companies:
Wega Film (Austria)
X-Filme (Germany)
Les Films du Losange (France)
Lucky Red (Italy)

Additional financing from:
Österreichisches Filminstitut
Filmfonds Wien
Deutscher Filmförderfonds
Filmförderungsanstalt
Medienboard Berlin-Brandenburg
Mitteldeutsche Medienförderung
Centre National de la
  Cinématographie (FR)
Eurimages

Television Partners:
ORF (Film/Fernseh-Abkommen)
Bayerischer Rundfunk
ARD/Degeto
France 3 Cinéma
TPS Star
Canal+TF1 Vidéo

Produced by:
Stefan Arndt
Veit Heiduschka
Michael Katz
Margaret Ménégoz
Andrea Occhipinti

Cast:
Christian Friedel (Teacher)
Ernst Jacobi (Voice of the aged teacher)
Leonie Benesch (Eva, the teacher's fiancée)
Ulrich Tukur (Baron)
Ursina Ladini (Marie-Louise, the
  baron's wife)
Fion Mutert (Sigi, the baron's son)
Burghart Klaußner (Pastor)
Steffi Kühnert (Anna, the pastor's wife)
Maria-Victoria Dragus (Klara, the pastor's
  daughter)
Leonard Proxauf (Martin, the pastor's son)
Rainer Bock (Doctor)
Roxane Duran (Anna, the doctor's
  daughter)
Susanne Lothar (Frau Emilia Wagner,
  the midwife)
Eddy Grahl (Karli, her disabled son)
Josef Bierbichler (Steward)
Gabriela Maria Schmeide (Emma, the
  steward's wife)
Janina Fautz (Erna, the steward's daughter)
Branko Samarovski (Peasant)
Aaron Denkel (Kurti, the peasant's son)
Birgit Minichmayr (Frieda, the peasant's
  daughter)

Music:
Franz Schubert, Variations on
  "Trockne Blumen" for flute & piano
  in E minor, D. 802 (Op. posth. 160)
Martin Luther, "Eine feste Burg ist unser
  Gott"
Paul Gerhardt, "Befiehl Du Deine
  Wege" (Bach BWV 244–53)

Cinematography:
Christian Berger

Film Editing:
Monika Willi

Set Design:
Christoph Kanter

Costume Design:
Moidele Bickel

Sound Design:
Guillaume Sciama
Jean-Pierre Laforce

Runtime:
144 min.

Sound Mix:
DTS/ Dolby Digital

Color:
Black-and-white

Aspect Ratio:
1.85:1

Film length:
4,000 m

Negative Format:
35 mm (Kodak Vision3 250D 5207,
    Vision3 500T 5219)

Camera:
Moviecam Compact, Cooke S4 Lenses

Cinematographic Process:
Digital Intermediate (2K) (master format)
    Super 35 (3-perf) (source format)

Printed Film Format:
35 mm (spherical) (Kodak 2302,
    Vision 2383) D-Cinema;
    E-Cinema

Production Costs:
12 million Euro

Release Dates:
May 21, 2009 (Cannes Film Festival)
September 17, 2009 (limited release
    in Germany)
September 24, 2009 (Austria)
October 15, 2009 (Germany)
December 30, 2009 (USA)

Prizes (Selection):
Palme d'Or 2009—Cannes
Golden Globe Awards—Best
    Foreign Language Film 2010
Oscar-Nominated for Best
    Foreign Language Film of the
    Year 2009
Cinema for Peace 2010—Award
    for Most Valuable Movie of
    the Year
European Film Prize in three
    categories (European Film,
    Directing, Screenplay)
Toronto Film Festival: Best Foreign
    Language Award, Hollywood
    World Award
Guldbagge Award—Best Foreign
    Language Film (Sweden)
Prix du Syndicat Français de la
    Critique 2009
Preis der deutschen Filmkritik 2009:
    Best Feature, Best Screenplay,
    Best Camera, Best Actor (Burghart
    Klaußner)

NOTES

1   See Thomas Elsaesser, "Performative Self-Contradictions: Michael Haneke's Mind Games," in *A Companion to Michael Haneke*, ed. Roy Grundmann (Malden, MA: Wiley-Blackwell, 2010), 53–74; Stewart Garrett, "Pre-War Trauma: Haneke's *The White Ribbon*," *Film Quarterly* 63, no. 4 (2010): 40–47, esp. 40.

2   See Haneke's interview with Karin Schiefer in her *Filmgespräche zum österreischischen Film* (Vienna: Synema, 2012), 6–11, as well as Jennifer M. Kapczynski's detailed treatment in "Raising Cain? The Logic of Breeding in Michael Haneke's 'Das weiße Band,'" *Colloquia Germanica* 43, no. 3 (2010): 153–73; esp. 155–56. Schiefer's interview is translated in *Michael Haneke: Interviews*, ed. Roy Grundmann, Fatima Naqvi, and Colin Root (Jackson: University Press of Mississippi, 2020), 110–15.

3   This literary device is found across many works from the late eighteenth through the nineteenth centuries. Some of them have been categorized as late Romantic fairy tales, others as poetic realist novellas. Examples range from Goethe's *Conversations of German Refugees* (*Unterhaltungen deutscher Ausgewanderten*, 1795) and Clemens Brentano's *Honor; or the Story of the Brave Caspar and the Fair Annerl* (*Geschichte vom braven Kasperl und dem schönen Annerl*, 1817) to Franz Grillparzer's *The Poor Musician* (*Der arme Spielmann*, 1848) and Conrad Ferdinand Meyer's *The Monk's Wedding* (*Die Hochzeit des Mönchs*, 1884). The technique is also common to Weimar cinema, e.g., Robert Wiene's *The Cabinet of Dr. Caligari* (1920) or F. W. Murnau's *Nosferatu* (1922).

4   Katharina Rutschky, ed. *Schwarze Pädagogik: Quellen zur Naturgeschichte der bürgerlichen Erziehung* (Frankfurt am Main: Ullstein Sachbuch, 1988).

5   The manipulative conventions of mainstream filmmaking are thematized in *Code inconnu* (2000) and the editing of digital TV "footage" in *Caché* (2005). Viewers are forced to reflect on the ethical implications of photojournalism, as well as on the way in which media have become invisible to their users. Haneke's 2017 film *Happy End* focuses on the Snapchat habits of the young protagonist (Fantine Harduin); we see the world through her smartphone lens.

6   Ingeborg Bachmann, *Three Paths to the Lake: Stories*, trans. Mary Fran Gilbert (New York: Holmes & Meier, 1989); "Drei Wege zum See," in *Simultan* (Munich: Piper, 1972), 130–205.

7   Sander's son published a larger selection of photographs in 1986, and the entirety was brought out in the new millennium. August Sander, *People of the Twentieth Century: A Cultural Work of Photographs Divided into Seven Groups*, ed. Susanne Lange, 7 vols. (Munich: Schirmer/Mosel, 2002); *Menschen des 20. Jahrhunderts: Ein Kulturwerk in Lichtbildern eingeteilt in sieben Gruppen*, ed. Susanne Lange, 7 vols. (Munich: Schirmer/Mosel, 2002).

8   See the documentary entitled *24 Wirklichkeiten in der Sekunde* (dir. Eva Testor and Nina Kusturica, 2005).

9   See Mary Ann Doane, "Indexicality and the Concept of Medium Specificity," in *The Meaning of Photography*, ed. Robin Kelsey and Blake Stimson (Williamstown: Sterling and Francine Clark Art Institute, 2008), 3–14, esp. 10.

10   James S. Williams, "Aberrations of Beauty: Violence and Cinematic Resistance in Haneke's *The White Ribbon*," in *Film Quarterly* 63, no. 4 (2010): 48–55, esp. 52.

11   His adaptation of playwright James Saunders' one-act drama *After Liverpool* (1974) is followed by a string of works of Austrian provenance. These include Ingeborg Bachmann's "Three Paths to the Lake" (1976), Peter Rosei's *Who Was Edgar Allan?* (1985), Joseph Roth's *Rebellion* (1993), Franz Kafka's *The Castle* (1997), and Elfriede Jelinek's *The Piano Teacher* (2001).

12   Karl Kraus, *The Last Days of Mankind: The Complete Text*, trans. Fred Bridgham (New Haven, CT: Yale University Press, 2015); *Die letzten Tage der Menschheit* (Frankfurt am Main: Suhrkamp, 1986).

13   Joseph Roth tells the story of a veteran lost in the First Austrian Republic. See Joseph Roth, *Rebellion*, trans. Michael Hoffmann (London: Granta, 2000).

14   Unlike *The Last Days of Mankind*, which roams from imperial capital to battlefield in the nearly 800-page-long collage of newspaper reports, war communiqués, and overheard conversations, Haneke remains focused on one locale.

15   Stefan Zweig, *Die Welt von gestern: Erinnerungen eines Europäers* (Frankfurt am Main: S. Fischer, 1992), 15.

16   For an analysis of the shots see James S. Williams, "Aberrations," 49–50, as well as Garrett, "Pre-War Trauma," 40–47.

17   The film ends in the church, where recruits with flower bouquets pinned to their lapels file into the first row. The young men get seats of honor in the front, displacing the town dignitaries customarily seated there during mass.

18   Williams, "Aberrations," 52.

19   Robert Musil, *The Man Without Qualities*, trans. Sophie Wilkins and Burton Pike (New York: Vintage, 1996), 55.

20   Thomas Elsaesser, *European Cinema and Continental Philosophy: Film as Thought Experiment* (New York: Bloomsbury Academic, 2019), 297.

21   Musil, *The Man Without Qualities*, 56.

22   See Haneke's detailed description of the processes used to create brilliantly sharp, digitally enhanced images in his interview with Cieutat and Rouyer in *Haneke über Haneke: Gespräche mit Michel Cietuat und Philippe Rouyer*, trans. Marcus Seibert (Berlin/Cologne: Alexander Verlag, 2013), 312–13.

23   Musil, *Man Without Qualities*, 56; cf. the German original, in *Der Mann ohne Eigenschaften* (Reinbek bei Hamburg: Rowohlt, 1978) 58.

24   Cf. Kapczynski, "Raising Cain," 158.

25   Haneke reviewed Bernhard's novel *Gargoyles* (*Verstörung*) for the daily newspaper *Die Presse* in 1967.

26   See Martin Jay, *Downcast Eyes: The Denigration of Vision in Twentieth-Century French Thought* (Berkeley: University of California Press, 1993).

27   Images are drawn directly from the film (no photographer produced separate stills) and the director approved the captions—so that film and extraneous materials form one continuous whole.

28   Haneke only secured funding in the new millennium after his other theatrical successes.

29   See Anne Whitehead, *Trauma Fiction* (Edinburgh: Edinburgh University Press, 2004), esp. 31–47.

30   See the German original: "Ich weiß nicht, ob die Geschichte, die ich Ihnen erzählen will, in allen Details der Wahrheit entspricht. Vieles darin weiß ich nur vom Hörensagen und manches weiß ich auch heute nach so vielen Jahren nicht zu enträtseln, und auf unzählige Fragen gibt es keine Antwort, aber dennoch glaube ich, dass ich die seltsamen Ereignisse, die sich in unserem Dorf zugetragen habe, erzählen muss, weil sie möglicherweise auf manche Vorgänge in diesem Land ein erhellendes Licht werfen können." In Michael Haneke, *Das weiße Band—Eine deutsche Kindergeschichte. Das Drehbuch zum Film* (Berlin: Berlin Verlag, 2009), 7, hereafter cited as *Drehbuch*; the screenplay is also reprinted in Michael Haneke, *Die Drehbücher* (Hamburg: Hoffmann und Campe, 2018) 891–1036.

31   According to an early plot synopsis in the Austrian Filmmuseum (WB 1252), the narrator was to be the steward's son Georg. This would have changed the vantage point: a total insider would have recounted the story. I consulted Haneke's material in the Austrian Filmmuseum (Österreichisches Filmmuseum) and have used its alphanumeric designations throughout.

32   Williams, "Aberrations," 48.

33   On the nineteenth-century realist tone, see Haneke's interview with Alexander Horwath, "The Haneke Code: Talking Shop, Theory and Practice with the Director of *The White Ribbon*," *Film Comment* 45, no. 6 (Nov.–Dec. 2009): 26–31, esp. 29.

34   WB 1252, 11.

35   Thomas Bernhard, *The Lime Works*, trans. Sophie Wilkins (New York: Vintage, 2010); *Das Kalkwerk*, in *Werke*, ed. Renate Langer, vol. 3 (Frankfurt am Main: Suhrkamp, 2004).

36   On the gradual fades see Garrett, "Pre-War Trauma," 47.

37   WB 1340.

38   See the essays collected in Bettine Menke and Thomas Glaser, ed., *Experimentalanordnungen der Bildung: Exteriorität—Theatralität—Literarizität* (Paderborn: Fink, 2014).

39   The translation of the subtitle was left out entirely in the internationally distributed version; global audiences were thus prevented from seeing the film as a solely Germanic affair. See Kapczynski, "Raising Cain," 156.

40 The credits come after a segment with deaf-mute children playing charades, who cannot interpret their classmate's pantomime. In later scenes, incomprehension is multiplied. Three different languages and dialects are spoken simultaneously and separate conversations intersect confusingly in a particularly paradigmatic sequence.

41 Carlo Ginzburg, "Clues: Roots of a Scientific Paradigm," *Theory and Society* 70, no. 3 (1979): 273–88, esp. 275

42 Rutschky's original reads: "eine Leerstelle, eine tabula rasa, die sich jeder Erzieher wünscht, um sich desto leichter in sie eintragen zu können" (*Schwarze Pädagogik*, li).

43 Rutschky, *Schwarze Pädagogik*, 148.

44 For a useful survey of this period, see chapters 5 ("Reconstruction and Integration: The Culture of West German Stabilization 1945 to 1968") and 6 ("The Federal Republic 1968 to 1990: From the Industrial Society to the Culture Society") in Rob Burns, ed., *German Cultural Studies: An Introduction* (New York: Oxford University Press, 1996), 209–323.

45 See the chronology in *Michael Haneke: Interviews*, esp. xx–xxi.

46 See Roy Grundmann's essay "Between Adorno and Lyotard: Michael Haneke's Aesthetic of Fragmentation," in *A Companion to Michael Haneke*, ed. Grundmann, 371–419, esp. 383–97.

47 Theodor W. Adorno, "The Meaning of Working Through the Past," 89–104; "Education After Auschwitz," 191–204; "On the Question: 'What is German?'," 205–14, in *Critical Models: Interventions and Catchwords* (New York: Columbia UP, 2005); "Was bedeutet: Aufarbeitung der Vergangenheit," 10–29; "Tabus über dem Lehrberuf," 73–91; "Erziehung nach Auschwitz," 92–109; "Erziehung zur Entbarbarisierung," 126–40 in *Erziehung zur Mündigkeit: Vorträge und Gespräche mit Hellmut Becker 1959–1969*, ed. Gerd Kadelbach (Frankfurt am Main: Suhrkamp, 1970). His "Tabus über dem Lehrberuf," 68–84; "Erziehung nach Auschwitz," 85–101; "Auf die Frage: Was ist deutsch," 102–12 are also in *Stichworte: Kritische Modelle* (Frankfurt am Main: Suhrkamp, 1998).

48 In this context, it is also worth mentioning that Ulrike Meinhof began her university studies in the discipline of pedagogy (*Pädagogik*) and psychology. See Jürgen Seifert, "Ulrike Meinhof," in *Die RAF und der linke Terrorismus*, ed. Wolfgang Kraushaar, vol. 1 (Hamburg: Hamburger Edition, 2006), 350–71, esp. 354.

49 WB 1252, 5–6.

50 Haneke, *Drehbuch*, 9.

51 Rutschky, too, follows the same tactics in attesting to textual violence. She takes bits out of context, montaging them under polemical subheadings such as "A Few Fantasies about *Erziehung* and the Profession of the Educator," "Training for Catastrophe," or "*Erziehung* as Rationalization of Sadism."

52 Rutschky, *Schwarze Pädagogik*, 192–98.

53 See J. B. Basedow and J. H. Campe, *Pädagogische Unterhandlungen* (Dessau: Crusius,

1777), vol. 4. See also Rutschky's section "Erziehung als Triebabwehr," *Schwarze Pädagogik*, 299–375, esp. 321–22.

54 Rutschky, *Schwarze Pädagogik*, 433–37, esp. 437.

55 This contraption was invented by D. G. M. Schreber to "enforce a lying posture during sleep" around 1858. See Rutschky fig. 29, p. 434.

56 Michael Rothberg, *Multidirectional Memory: Remembering the Holocaust in the Age of Decolonization* (Palo Alto, CA: Stanford University Press, 2009).

57 Rothberg, *Multidirectional Memory*, 2–7, esp. 7. See his chapter on Haneke's *Caché*, esp. 267–308.

58 Rothberg, *Multidirectional Memory*, 7, 14.

59 See, for example, Adorno, "Erziehung nach Auschwitz," in *Erziehung zur Mündigkeit*, 99.

60 Kapczynski, "Raising Cain," 156, 161.

61 Peter Kümmel, "Von diesen Kindern stammen wir ab?," *Die Zeit*, 8 Oct. 2009. https://www.zeit.de/2009/42/Das-weisse-Band (accessed 4 May 2020).

62 On this issue see Alan Robinson, *Narrating the Past: Historiography, Memory and the Contemporary Novel* (New York: Palgrave, 2011), 150.

63 WB 1252, esp. 1.

64 See in particular Dagmar Herzog's chapters on "The Fragility of Heterosexuality" (64–100) and "The Morality of Pleasure" (141–83) in her *Sex after Fascism: Memory and Morality in Twentieth-Century Germany* (Princeton, NJ: Princeton University Press, 2007).

65 WB 1252, 6.

66 Women such as the mother in *Benny's Video* or the adoptive mother in *71 Fragments of a Chronology of Chance* are the ones most likely to show empathy in stressful situations.

67 See Theweleit's discussion of Meinhof's radicalization in *Ghosts: Drei leicht inkorrekte Vorträge* (Stroemfeld/Roter Stern, 1998), 22–25, 31–33. See also Mario Krebs, *Ulrike Meinhof: Ein Leben im Widerspruch* (Reinbek: Rowohlt, 1989), 16–28; Jürgen Seifert, "Ulrike Meinhof," 350–71, and Susanne Bressan and Martin Jander, "Gudrun Ensslin," 398–429, as well as Jörg Herrmann, "'Unsere Söhne, unsere Töchter': Protestantismus und RAF-Terrorismus in den 1970-er Jahren," 644–56, all in *Die RAF und der linke Terrorismus*, ed. Wolfgang Kraushaar, vol. 1 (Hamburg: Hamburger Edition, 2006).

68 Haneke, *Drehbuch*, 16.

69 See Richard Wigmore's English translation: "All you flowers / that she gave to me, / you shall be laid / with me in the grave," https://www.oxfordlieder.co.uk/song/2061 (accessed 12 May 2020).

70 Klaus Theweleit, *Male Fantasies: Women, Floods, Bodies, History*, trans. Stephan Conway (Minneapolis: University of Minnesota Press, 1987); *Männerphantasien* (Frankfurt am Main: Roter Stern, 1977).

71 See Sven Reichardt's analysis of Theweleit's importance for the West German Left in his "Klaus Theweleits 'Männerphantasien'—ein Erfolgsbuch der 1970er-Jahre," *Zeithistorische Forschungen/Studies in Contemporary History*, Online-Edition, 3 (2006): 401–21, esp. 402, 405, https://zeithistorische-forschungen.de/3-2006/4650 (accessed 25 May 2020).

72 Haneke, *Drehbuch*, 182.

73 WB 1252, esp. 5–6.

74 Haneke writes: "Ich möchte eine Gruppe von jungen Menschen zeigen, die in einem scheinbar festgefügten Ordnungssystem die Prinzipien dieser Ordnung in kindlichem Idealismus verabsolutieren, sich zu Hütern dieser Ideale und damit zu Richtern über die vor ihnen Versagenden machen und damit die vollkommene Pervertierung eben dieser Ideale exemplarisch vorführen" (WB 1252, 5).

75 Haneke continues: "Wer als der Stärkere kraft (Spiel-)Autorität eingesetzt wird, hat die Macht. Wer die Macht hat, dem muß gehorcht werden. Wer nicht gehorcht, ist schlecht. Wer schlecht ist, muß bestraft werden" (WB 1252, 6).

76 See the materials collected in WB 999, 990, 1008.

77 See Adorno's essay "On the Question: 'What is German?,'" 205–14.

78 WB 1004.

79 See Sander's reprinted foreword, in August Sander, *Menschen des 20. Jahrhunderts: Portraitphotographie von 1892–1952* (Munich: Schirmer Mosel, 1980), n.p.

80 Reprinted: August Sander, *Antlitz der Zeit: Sechzig Aufnahmen deutscher Menschen des 20. Jahrhunderts*. Foreword by Alfred Döblin (Munich: Schirmer/Mosel, 2003).

81 Walter Benjamin, *Deutsche Menschen*, in *Gesammelte Schriften*, ed. Tillman Rexroth, vol. IV.2 (Frankfurt am Main: Suhrkamp, 1991), 149–234, esp. 150.

82 Brian Britt, *Postsecular Benjamin: Agency and Tradition* (Evanston, IL: Northwestern University Press, 2016), 158–59.

83 See Haneke's interviews with Geoff Andrew in "The Revenge of the Children," *Sight & Sound* XIX.12 (Dec. 2009): 14–17, esp. 15; and in great detail with Rouyer and Cieutat in *Haneke über Haneke*, esp. 317–18. Haneke's casting directors were Markus Schleinzer, a filmmaker and actor, and Carmen Loley.

84 Döblin, "Von Gesichten," 12–13; 13–14.

85 Döblin, "Von Gesichten," 12–13.

86 Cf. Elizabeth Büttner and Christian Dewald, eds., *Anschluß an Morgen: Eine Geschichte des österreichischen Films von 1945 bis zur Gegenwart* (Vienna: Residenz Verlag, 1997), 306–27.

87 See Adorno's "Education after Auschwitz," 196, and "Erziehung nach Auschwitz," in *Erziehung zur Mündigkeit*, 98; the German means "flat land."

88 Sander's landscape photos—far less known than his portraits—document the particu-

larity of an area or the small details of a special place. The photographer made tourist brochures for regional agencies seeking to increase local travel after World War I, with many close-ups and medium shots of trees, paths, and plants near his home.

89　In Haneke's films *Funny Games* (1997) and *Funny Games U.S.* (2007), the latter a shot-by-shot remake of the former, the youthful murderers are presented as outgrowths of their environment rather than an evil that enters from the outside.

90　Once the doctor and midwife have disappeared from Eichwald, the camera focuses our attention on the town's deserted streets. In post-production, all traces of modern-day life were erased, and we are left with a postcard idyll, a picturesque town from which the supposed perpetrators have withdrawn after their malfeasance is uncovered.

91　A series of reminiscences punctuate the story's progression and lend it a fragmentary structure. About twenty-five minutes into the film, we see a series of pictures in a dreamlike flashback, which is interrupted by another flashback. After zooming in on a portrait of Elisabeth as a young girl, the film dissolves to one black-and-white photo of her after the next. The narrator recounts her career from humble beginnings to the successful present, going chronologically from portrait to portrait.

92　Susan Sontag, *On Photography* (New York: Picador, 1977), 180.

93　Trotta's concerns recur verbatim in Haneke's *Code inconnu* (2000), where one figure is also a photojournalist (Thierry Neuvic).

94　We might think of the overlapping of National Socialism and the critique of late capitalism in *Benny's Video* and *Funny Games*, for instance, or the American invasion of Iraq and the Paris massacre of Oct. 17, 1961 in *Caché*.

95　Susan Sontag, *Regarding the Pain of Others* (New York: Picador, 2003), 113–15.

96　On this aspect, see Claudia Breger's extended analysis of Haneke's "'localized' techniques of narration" that utilize historical affect in her chapter "Tenderly Cruel Realisms: Objectfull Assembly and the Horizon of a Shared World" in *Making Worlds: Affect and Collectivity in Contemporary European Cinema* (New York: Columbia University Press, 2020), 155–98, esp. 162–74.

97　In Haneke's *Amour* (2012), photomontages of the elderly couples' empty apartment interrupt the unfolding story. After Anne (Emmanuelle Riva) has a stroke and is hospitalized, the montage of eighteenth- and nineteenth-century landscape paintings makes palpable her absence and impending death.

98　See "'Schwarz-Weiß ist ja viel schöner': Ein Gespräch der Bildwelten des Wissens mit dem Regisseur Michael Haneke," interview with Violeta Sánchez in *Bildwelten des Wissens: Graustufen*, ed. Claudia Blümle et al. (Berlin: De Gruyter, 2011), 86–101; Susanne Schmetkamp, "Perspektive und empathische Resonanz: Vergegenwärtigung anderer Sichtweisen," in *Empathie im Film: Perspektiven der Ästhetischen Theorie, Phänomenologie und Analytischen Philosophie*, ed. Malte Hagener and Íngrid Vendrell Ferran (Bielefeld: Transcript, 2017), 133–66; and *Haneke über Haneke*, 313. A full list in the archive shows Haneke's digital changes to light sources, making microphones invisible, deleting any signs of breath from the corpse, etc. (WB 1001).

99 Daniel Varndell, "The Enigma of *The White Ribbon*," in *New Review of Film and Television Studies* 15, no. 1 (2017): 108–20, esp. 114.

100 Interestingly enough, the film begins with a white scarf—a ribbon-like piece of fabric—drifting into blackish water and is punctuated by hanging white sheets with clues written on them in blood.

101 She is certainly not the only one linked to the cross. Her brother in his bed watches a cinematic scene on the wall of his room formed by the "projected" light from the fire; the doctor is seen against the cross of the window's mullions; after the young farmer discovers his hanged father, we see the cross of the timbered frame behind him.

102 *Drehbuch*, 136.

103 See note 67. In addition, see Jörg Herrmann, "Ulrike Meinhof und Gudrun Ensslin—Vom Protestantismus zum Terrorismus," in *Zur Vorstellung des Terrors: Die RAF*, ed. Klaus Biesenbach (Berlin: Steidl, 2005), 112–14.

104 See Theweleit's analysis of this language reduction in his "Bemerkungen zum RAF-Gespenst: 'Abstrakter Radikalismus' und Kunst," in *Ghosts*, esp. 19–20, 34.

105 Theweleit, "Bemerkungen," 52–53, 18.

106 WB 1252, 2.

107 Theweleit, "Bemerkungen," 57.

108 His first three films for the cinema, *The Seventh Continent* (*Der siebente Kontinent*, 1989), *Benny's Video* (1992), and *71 Fragments of a Chronology of Chance* (*71 Fragmente einer Chronologie des Zufalls*, 1994) have often been referred to as the "Glaciation Trilogy."

109 Cf. Adorno, "Education after Auschwitz," 192, 200–203.

110 Luther's lyrics are taken from Charles Seymour Robinson, ed., *Psalms & Hymns, & Spiritual Songs: A Manual of Worship for The Church of Christ* (New York: A. S. Barnes, 1876), esp. 165. My thanks to Sophie Duvernoy for pointing out the choral element. Viewers may associate the lyrics with the narrator's efforts to pry open the community's insularity and smugness by telling this tale. Church services punctuate the film, but this final shot is the only one to give us an encompassing view of the interior space and the assembled. The camera is centrally located across from the entryway, through which people file. The entrance turns black when everyone is seated, producing a dark and ominous vortex in the center. The soundtrack continues mournfully, fading out with the last verse of the first stanza. The blackness radiates outward from the central vanishing point, engulfing everything.

111 This inversion was present in the harvest festival, where the "festive" atmosphere turned to "dread" and "perplexity," as the narrator stated.

112 Thanks to set designer Alex McCargar for noting this.

113 A. O. Scott, "Wholesome Hamlet's Horror Sends a Jolt to the System," *New York Times*, 29 Dec. 2009. https://www.nytimes.com/2009/12/30/movies/30white.html (accessed 25 May 2020).

114 *The White Ribbon* suggests that there are limits to the translatability of events into other cultural contexts—a film like this can only partially work through overlaps with other moments of ideological indoctrination.

Printed in the United States
By Bookmasters